★ HOW TO BE *Wild* LIKE ★
KEITH RICHARDS

Published by Marshall Cavendish Editions
An imprint of Marshall Cavendish International
1 New Industrial Road, Singapore 536196

Other Marshall Cavendish Offices: Marshall Cavendish International.
PO Box 65829, London EC1P 1NY, UK • Marshall Cavendish Corporation.
99 White Plains Road, Tarrytown NY 10591-9001, USA • Marshall Cavendish
International (Thailand) Co Ltd. 253 Asoke, 12th Flr, Sukhumvit 21 Road,
Klongtoey Nua, Wattana, Bangkok 10110, Thailand • Marshall Cavendish
(Malaysia) Sdn Bhd, Times Subang, Lot 46, Subang Hi-Tech Industrial Park,
Batu Tiga, 40000 Shah Alam, Selangor Darul Ehsan, Malaysia.

Marshall Cavendish is a trademark of Times Publishing Limited

National Library Board, Singapore Cataloguing-in-Publication Data

Wilson, Jack, 1962-
How to be wild like Keith Richards : 50 years of riffs, spliffs, snorting & soul
from the original wild man of rock 'n' roll / Jack Wilson. — Singapore : Marshall
Cavendish Editions, c2011.
p. cm.
ISBN : 978-981-4346-48-1 (pbk.)

1. Richards, Keith, 1943- 2. Rock musicians — England — Biography.
3. Rolling Stones. I. Title.

ML420.R515
782.42166092 -- dc22   OCN720122008

Printed in Singapore by Times Printers

★ HOW TO BE *Wild* LIKE ★
KEITH RICHARDS

50 Years of **RIFFS, SPLIFFS, SNORTING & SOUL** from the Original Wild Man of Rock 'n' Roll

JACK WILSON

Marshall Cavendish Editions

For my friends and family
You guys are the perfect backing group.

Thanks for providing many years
of beautiful harmonies, happy handclaps,
delicious doowopshowaddywaddies and
a whole lot of rock 'n' roll.

ACKNOWLEDGEMENTS

I'd like to thank the wonderful people at Marshall Cavendish for their time, patience, professionalism and cake. I'm especially grateful to Stephanie Yeo, Lynn Chin, Melvin Neo, Violet Phoon, Sanae Inada and Chris Newson.

I'm also grateful to the amazing team at PodTribe.com for taking on the e-edition of the book. Special thanks to Mike and Monette Hamlin, Maysie Lagman, John Gonzalez and Karen Azupardo.

I'd like to thank Nury Vittachi, Steve Dawson and Glenn Conley for their useful feedback, dry comments, wicked wit and whisky chasers.

As always, the encore goes to Mum and Dad — for always being supportive, encouraging, open-minded and forgiving.

CONTENTS

INTRODUCTION

Jack Wilson here. I thought I should mention that this book is completely unauthorised. **KEITH RICHARDS** isn't even aware of my existence. He had nothing to do with it. It just happens to be about him. To clarify matters, Keith Richards was not harmed or abused in any way in the making of this book. At least not by me. Knowing Keith as I do, in the figurative sense obviously, not the literal, I suspect that at some time during the period of writing this book there was a certain amount of abuse going on in his life but for Keith it wouldn't be seen to be abuse in the same way as others see it. I mean, when **DRUGS** and **ALCOHOL** form an inherent part of your life so that it's almost a part of your personality, is it still abuse? I don't think so. So for fans of Keith out there you can relax and enjoy the book. While Keith is oblivious to the making of this book I hope that one day one of his mates will look out from over his **JACK DANIELS** and say "Hey Keith, did you see that book that some English guy wrote about you? It's called *HOW TO BE WILD LIKE KEITH RICHARDS* and it talks all about the weird drunken stoner bollox that went on in your life and then it goes on to describe all those other weird and wild dudes that tore through the **'60s, '70s, AND '80s** and Keith will probably give him one of those deep-throated, rasping chuckles of his and say, "Cheeky bastard, I hope he chokes on the nib of his pen", because Keith is surprisingly literary and is also a big fan of my favourite novelist George Macdonald Fraser, you know, the guy who wrote the **FLASHMAN** books. Bloody funny. So we do have something in common. We both read George Macdonald Fraser and have a strong interest in history. I never really did drugs though so I guess that makes us a bit different. There's some good stuff in here too about weird **SCANDINAVIAN BLACK METAL** and other dudes who sold their soul for rock 'n' roll. Literally. They really screwed up their report card with the Big Fella upstairs. Then of course there's the crazies — **KEITH MOON** is my favourite. Moon the Loon. There's some stuff about him and other stuff about groupies but I didn't put in the Jimi Hendrix and the **PLASTERCASTERS** story cos everyone knows that one. I was going to put in the story about **LED ZEPPELIN** and the groupie with the fish but that was kinda gross and I don't want the RSPCA coming after me for promoting cruelty to animals. So on that low fish note I should probably wrap this up. Oh but hang on a moment I should also mention that there's some really **GREAT QUOTES** from some of music's big names, some links to useful websites and **CAMERON DIAZ** gets a passing mention. I hope you readers out there get a kick out of this book. I certainly enjoyed getting to know Keith and his buddies. What a jolly interesting bunch they turned out to be! Until next time, *mis amigos*. Ciao and cheers. **JACK WILSON**.

Britain is home to some of the greatest creative talents the world has ever seen... from Shakespeare, Wordsworth, Coleridge and Keats, to Kipling, Orwell, Wilde and Olivier; but it has somehow also managed to produce creative geniuses with an equally destructive edge. The Chinese believe in Yin and Yang — a balance in life. Sometimes these balances swing to the furthest extremes of the pendulum... a good case in point being Mr Keith Richards. To misquote Shakespeare (rather badly):

> Some are born wild
> Some Achieve wildness
> And some have wildness
> thrust upon them

Keith Richards didn't so much have wildness thrust upon him as track it down, invite it for dinner, feed it toxic substances and embrace it as his best buddy.

Keith Richards, or Keef as he's affectionately known in the British press, was born 18 December 1943 in the middle of one of history's greatest periods of mayhem — the Second World War.

"I'M A SAGITTARIUS, HALF-MAN, HALF-HORSE, WITH A LICENSE TO SHIT IN THE STREET."

In his early years, Keith showed an interest in music and at the age of 12 even sang the Hallelujah Chorus in Westminster Abbey for the Queen. Keith called it his "first taste of showbiz". Soon afterwards Keith entered his teenage years and began a difficult time in his life. He hated school and was often involved in fights with other kids from his own school or a rival school nearby. At this point his grandfather, Gus Dupree, encouraged him to learn the guitar and expand his interest in American rock 'n' roll. Gus had actually been a talented musician and band leader himself and was described by Keith as "the funkiest old coot you could ever meet".

In 1959, after many warnings, Keith was eventually expelled from school. Rather than just kick him out, the headmaster suggested he might find a niche as an artist, and Richards signed up for Sidcup Art School.

Fellow Sidcup student and future Pretty Things guitarist Dick Taylor remembers, "There was a lot of music being played at Sidcup, and we'd go into the empty classrooms and fool around with our guitars. ... Even in those days Keith could play most of [Chuck Berry's] solos." He also mentions that Keith "... was a real Ted, just a hooligan".

In between lessons at Sidcup, Keith decided to share his newfound knowledge of drugs with the local wildlife. "In order to stay up late with our music and still get to Sidcup in the morning, Keith and I were on a pretty steady diet of pep pills, which not only kept us awake but gave us a lift. We took all kinds of things — pills that girls took for menstruation, inhalers like Nostrilene, and other stuff.

Opposite the college there was this little park with an aviary that had a cockatoo in it. Cocky the Cockatoo we used to call it. Keith used to feed it pep pills and make it stagger around on its perch. If ever we were feeling bored we'd go and give another upper to Cocky."

"Keith is the kind of guy you should leave alone. He is the classic naughty schoolboy, the sort of guy I knew at school who hated the Head Boy. And I loved Keith because of that."

Charlie Watts

Keith and Mick Jagger had both attended Wentworth Primary School in Dartford, Kent and met again years later on a train in 1960 when Jagger was attending the London School of Economics. The two discovered they had a common interest in American R&B, especially for the music of Chuck Berry, Muddy Waters and Robert Johnson. Both of them soon put their studies to one side and focused on their music careers.

Their first band was called **Little Boy Blue and the Blue Boys** — not exactly a name to lead the bill at Knebworth. The name was soon changed to The Rolling Stones, after a song by Muddy Waters. On 12 July 1962 the group played their first formal gig at the Marquee Club, billed as **The Rollin' Stones**. The line-up was Mick Jagger, Keith Richards, Brian Jones, Ian Stewart on piano, Mick Taylor on bass and Tony

Chapman on drums. Bass guitarist Bill Wyman replaced Mick Taylor in December and drummer Charlie Watts joined the following January to form the Stones' rhythm section. Wyman has always maintained that the only reason he was asked to join the Stones is that he owned an amp that was badly needed by the band at that time.

In 1962 Brian, Keith and Mick moved into an apartment in London. There was never enough money for heating in the winter so the guys often used to just hang out in bed together. John Lennon once went over and found Keith and Mick in bed together and often said he was unsure about their sexuality.

In fact, their lifestyle very much reflected the 'free love' movement of the '60s. They shared everything: hotel rooms, beds and even partners. Perhaps the most pointed example of this is the extremely wild and promiscuous Anita Pallenberg, but more of her later...

In the early days, the band was led by Brian Jones, who was an exceptional musician with an instinctive feel for the Blues... a remarkable achievement for a blonde, middle-class Englishman from Cheltenham.

Jones was to influence the early Stones in many ways, from music to lifestyle to wild man. By the age of 21 he had already fathered three children out of wedlock and was an experienced drug user. He was also very much the band's leader. Watts described Jones' role in these early days: "Brian was very instrumental in pushing the band at the beginning. Keith and I would look at him and say he was barmy. It was a crusade to him to get us on the stage in a club and be paid a half-crown and to be billed as an R&B band."

The group played at blues and jazz clubs, building a large following at the Crawdaddy Club in Richmond. While Jagger was lead singer, Jones, at this time, was very much the leader — promoting the band, getting shows, and negotiating with club owners.

Keith was already a talented musician but he was constantly experimenting with different guitar styles. He and Jones formed a formidable partnership and drew their inspiration from many of the leading US R&B stars. Keith and Brian developed a style of playing together that Keith called guitar weaving. **"WE LISTENED TO THE TEAMWORK, TRYING TO WORK OUT WHAT WAS GOING ON IN THOSE RECORDS; HOW YOU COULD PLAY TOGETHER WITH TWO GUITARS AND MAKE IT SOUND LIKE FOUR OR FIVE."**

Even in these early days Keith was establishing a reputation as a wild boy. The Stones' first manager, Georgio Gomelsky, said: "Keith has never grown up in my opinion. He's always at war. He's too much. He's a rubbery kind of person, he bounces off anything and then he comes back. Nobody knows how he does it, he's always there. He's a very great character."

Sadly the same could not be said of George's business skills and in 1963 he was replaced by a sharp young agent called Andrew Loog Oldham. Only 19 years old and described by

> "DESPITE THE 'PELVIS' TAG, NOBODY HAD REALLY FELT THREATENED BY ELVIS, BUT HERE WERE FIVE OF THEM [THE STONES], AND THEY WEREN'T PROPOSING TO HOLD YOUR DAUGHTER'S HAND, THEY WANTED TO SPEND THE NIGHT TOGETHER. OH GOD!"
> — CARL HIAASEN

George Melly as "calculatedly vicious and nasty, but pretty as a stoat", it was Oldham who would shape the Stones over the next few years and establish them as one of the greatest bands of the era.

According to Richards he was "a fantastic bullshitter and an incredible hustler". In contrast with the Beatles' neat suits and ties and cheeky scouse appeal, Oldham encouraged The Stones to wear their hair long and their clothes loud. He also came up with the slogan *"Would You Let Your Daughter Go Out with a Rolling Stone?"*.

On top of creating a new look for the band, Oldham also revolutionised their music by forcing Mick and Keith to write their own songs. Up until this point, the Stones had been content to play cover versions of other people's hits.

1964

MAY: Their first album — *The Rolling Stones* — reached #1. Their concerts at this time contrasted sharply with the concerts of previous years and often ended in a riot. **"IT WAS LIKE THEY HAD THE BATTLE OF THE CRIMEA GOING ON. PEOPLE GASPING, TITS HANGING OUT, CHICKS CHOKING, NURSES RUNNING AROUND WITH AMBULANCES. YOU TOOK YOUR LIFE IN YOUR HANDS JUST TO WALK OUT THERE. I WAS STRANGLED TWICE."**

– KEITH

Later that year, the Stones flew across the pond for their first-ever US tour. They also released their first US album with the snappy title *England's Newest Hit Makers*. (In retrospect, Andrew Loog Oldham may not have been the marketing genius that he claimed to be!) They also cemented their reputation as the bad boys of rock 'n' roll when their fans rioted on *The Ed Sullivan Show*.

1965 The rioting continues in Australia when 3,000 fans turn up to welcome them at the airport. On their return home their single *The Last Time* goes to #1 and the band are caught and fined for peeing against a wall at a petrol station in London.

1967 Ed Sullivan's outrage at the title of their song, *Let's Spend the Night Together*, results in the Stones having to perform the song as *Let's Spend Some Time Together*. On 12 February, police raid Keith's house Redlands in West Wittering and Keith and Mick are charged with drug possession.

" His moves are invariably graceful, well struck, and he makes sense of the body rhetoric that is the most classic, most fitting for a guitar rocker. He's the discus thrower of rock. He's perfect. "
— Pete Townshend, The Who

Oldham was replaced as manager in 1967 by Allan Klein and although he stayed on for a while as their producer, relations between him and the band became strained. His bizarre behaviour and excessive drug habit became too much even for the Stones.

The Oldham era was important in many ways for the Stones. Perhaps the most significant effect was to diminish the role and influence of Brian Jones and bring Mick and Keith to the centre of the stage. Oldham pushed Jagger to assume the lead role in the band, forcing Jones to take a back seat. The new Jagger/Richards writing combination also forced Jones to take a lesser role as there was little room for the cover versions that were Jones' speciality.

This effect on Jones was catastrophic and led to a rapid decline in his behaviour. His use of drugs spiralled out of control and he became increasingly alienated from the band. As Bill Wyman observed in *Stone Alone*:

"THERE WERE TWO BRIANS... ONE WAS INTROVERTED, SHY, SENSITIVE, DEEP-THINKING... THE OTHER WAS A PREENING PEACOCK, GREGARIOUS, ARTISTIC, DESPERATELY NEEDING ASSURANCE FROM HIS PEERS... HE PUSHED EVERY FRIENDSHIP TO THE LIMIT AND WAY BEYOND."

As Jones became increasingly bitter about the power shift in the band, his contributions began to decline. Instead of playing a major role in the creative work of the band, he was reduced to playing exotic background instruments.

To further rub salt in the wound, his girlfriend **Anita Pallenberg** ditched him in 1967 for Keith. The band had made a trip to Morocco and Brian allegedly attacked Pallenberg before falling sick and being hospitalised.

Keith did his White Knight bit and saved Pallenberg, then proceeded to bed her and embark on one of rock 'n' roll's most devastating partnerships. What Keith probably needed at this point in his life was someone to bring a bit of stability. Instead, the pernicious Pallenberg came along and stoked the self-destructive flames of Keith Richards.

"IT WAS A VERY COLD-BLOODED AFFAIR," Keith said of the split.

The decline of Brian Jones from this point on is one of rock 'n' roll's sadder stories. Although still officially a member of the Stones, he gradually contributed less and less. His mood swings and drug habit made him more of a liability than an asset. Sometimes in the recording studio his guitar would simply be switched off, leaving Keith to record all the guitar parts. According to biographer Gary Herman, Jones was "literally incapable of making music; when he tried to play harmonica, his mouth started bleeding".

1969 Jagger would later say that "[Firing Brian] had to be done because we felt we needed someone, and he wasn't there. He wouldn't come to the studio. He wouldn't do anything. We felt we couldn't go on. In fact, we came to a point where we couldn't play live. We couldn't hold our heads up and play because Brian was a total liability. He wasn't playing well, wasn't playing at all, couldn't hold the guitar. It was pathetic."

In June 1969 the Stones told Jones that he was no longer required and that he was to be replaced by Mick Taylor, a talented guitarist formerly with John Mayall's

Bluesbreakers. One month later Jones was dead, found drowned at the bottom of his swimming pool. Jones' death at 27 marked the founding of the 27 Club, otherwise known as the Forever 27 Club. This club is for musicians who have died at the age of 27 — evidently more than you would imagine. The original list of club members was Brian Jones, Jimi Hendrix, Janis Joplin and Jim Morrison. Many years later, Kurt Cobain of Nirvana would join the club. Some significance is also placed by some screwballs on the fact that four of the five original members were carrying white lighters with them at the time of their death.

Other less famous musicians who are members of the Forever 27 Club include Alan "Blind Owl" Wilson of Canned Heat, Arlester "Dyke" Christian of Dyke and the Blazers, Ron "Pigpen" McKernan of the Grateful Dead, Fat Pat of Screwed Up Click and Freaky Tah of Lost Boyz. (I mention these artists for no other reason other than they have really cool names.)

Two days after Jones' death, the Stones played a concert in Hyde Park, London as a tribute to Jones. The concert was a resounding success so it was decided they should play another free tribute concert in California a few months later. This concert was plagued by problems from the beginning. The venue itself was even moved twice before being settled in Altamont, a speedway track outside of San Francisco.

The Grateful Dead, who were due to play at the concert, recommended that Hell's Angels be used as security. The decision proved to be a disaster, the mistake being compounded by the fact that the Angels were to be paid with US$500 worth of beer.

The concert began in the afternoon with Santana, who were followed on stage by Jefferson Airplane. There was trouble throughout both sets and the Jefferson Airplane set ended prematurely when lead singer Marty Balin was knocked out as he tried to break up a particularly vicious fight. The trouble continued throughout the following acts until eventually night came and the Stones took the stage. From the opening lines of *Jumpin' Jack Flash*, there was serious trouble. The Hell's Angels were picking fight after fight with members of the crowd and eventually turned on Meredith Hunter, a stoned 18-year-old black youth who was there with his blonde girlfriend. There's some debate about exactly what happened but Hunter drew a gun in self defence and got off one shot before being viciously beaten and stabbed to death.

Unaware of what had happened but realising that it was impossible to carry on, the Stones fled the stage and flew off in a waiting helicopter. If Woodstock marked the pinnacle of the '60s Peace Movement, then Altamont marked the end.

American analyst Albert Goldman commented at the time: "What has emerged from their triumphal progress... is a public image of sado-homosexual-junkie-diabolic-sarcastic-nigger-evil unprecedented in the annals of pop culture."

1970 The Stones were under contractual obligation to provide Decca with a single. Under protest they supplied them with *Cocksucker Blues*. This was also the name of an unreleased documentary made about the Stones by director Robert Frank two years later. The documentary covered the Stones' tour of North America and was banned from release by a court order. Of course this hasn't stopped it from sneaking onto YouTube...

For a band that prided itself on being down and dirty, the Stones made a surprising appointment in the form of the decidedly upper-crusty Prince Rupert Loewenstein as their business manager.

This was also the year that Mick Jagger performed in Nicolas Roeg's widely acclaimed film *Performance* with Keith's girlfriend Anita Pallenberg.

"Everybody gets fucked up sooner or later. You're just pretending if you don't let your music get as liquid as you are when you're high."

Neil Young

Mick marries Bianca Perez Morena de Macias in St Tropez. The Stones became tax exiles and took up residence at a former Gestapo headquarters in the South of France called Nellcote. The months they stayed there provided more than enough material for Robert Greenfield's extremely entertaining classic, *Exile on Main Street: A Season in Hell With the Rolling Stones*. You have to warm to an author who takes time off from telling his story to taunt rival biographers along the way: "Memo to Stephen Davis, author of *Old Gods Almost Dead: The 40-Year Odyssey of the Rolling Stones*: It was not, as you incorrectly wrote in your book, the 'overweight, glamour-deprived Gram Parsons' whom Keith threw out of his room in Denver after 'Gram threatened Keith with a knife after having been denied all the cocaine in the room...', it was Stephen Stills. Next time you want to check a fact about the Stones, please feel free to call me in the office."

One of the things that put a bit of a bit of a damper on the recording sessions was that Keith and Mick weren't on the best of terms. While they were at Nellcote, Anita Pallenberg discovered she was pregnant. Nothing wrong with that, except for the fact that she suspected it might be Mick's baby. Rumour has it that Mick and Anita had a fling on the set of the Nicolas Roeg film, *Performance*. Insiders certainly seem convinced that something happened.

Due to the tension between Keith and Mick... and the fact that everything would grind to a halt while Keith and Anita shot up with heroin in their room... and a fire on the mattress where Anita and Keith were sleeping... and allegations that Anita had given heroin to the teenage daughter of the chef... and numerous police raids... and the theft of all the band's guitars by some of their drug suppliers... it was a miracle that *Exile on Main Street* was released at all.

With the French police closing in on the group, the Stones fled the country and Anita went to Switzerland to give birth to their daughter. While there, Keith and Anita entered a clinic to try and shake their heroin addiction. In fact, over the next few years they would each try a variety of methods to go clean. One of Keith's attempts received particular attention in the media since it allegedly involved checking into a Swiss clinic and having his blood transfused through a filter in a form of dialysis that cleansed the blood. While this may be true, the story somehow became exaggerated over the years until the media had Keith changing his blood on a regular basis.

In the words of the notoriously unreliable biography from Stones' hanger-on, Spanish Tony: **"I COULDN'T HELP WONDERING WHERE ALL THIS BLOOD WAS COMING FROM OR RESENTING THE DECADENCE OF DEBAUCHED MILLIONAIRES REGAINING THEIR HEALTH, VAMPIRE-LIKE, FROM THE FRESH CLEAN BLOOD OF INNOCENTS."**

A curiously ethical standpoint from the Stones' chief drug supplier!

1972 The band went to Jamaica to record their next album, *Goat's Head Soup*. The recording of the album was interrupted by the French police who issued a warrant for Keith's arrest. The whole band had to return to France to face charges. "A very sensible magistrate saw that I'd walked into my house, which I'd rented to a lot of people who'd been very clumsy and not cleaned up after themselves. The cops even tried to string in this old Belgian shotgun that was built in 1899... The police tried their damnedest to tell this 'ere magistrate that this weapon was a sawn-off shotgun. From that moment on the magistrate saw what was happening." Keith was fined US$300.

At the celebration party afterwards, Keith fell asleep in one of the hotel bedrooms and his cigarette set fire to a bed. As usual with Keith, the party ended in chaos with screaming and swearing and smoke.

Keith has been present at a number of fires in his lifetime, including a couple in his own home of Redlands in West Wittering. When asked about how he keeps the home fires burning he said, "It's a combustible bastard. It's not the most pleasant experience, sitting in your joint and the fucker combusts..."

 1973 Keith's UK home in Redlands burns down again but he escapes safely with Anita and their kids.

Anita continued with her excessive drug usage and worked her way towards a physical and mental breakdown. Keith took up with Uschi Obermeier, a German überbabe... and sometime actress and model. Like all good Rolling Stones stories, Uschi started with dating Mick and ended up with Keith. It looked for a while as if Keith would leave Anita for Uschi but it was not to be.

"I NEVER KNEW HOW MUCH HE REALLY LOVED ME BECAUSE I TOOK IT MORE AS A KIND OF GAME. I HAD TOO MUCH RESPECT FOR ANITA THAT I WASN'T EVEN REALLY THINKING THAT I COULD TAKE HER PLACE... ALSO... IT WAS DIFFICULT BECAUSE WITH THEM MUSIC IS THE FIRST LOVE, SECOND PLACE COMES MUSIC AND ALSO THIRD PLACE, AND THEN IN FOURTH PLACE YOU MUST COME."

– USCHI

1974 The Stones went to Munich to record their new album, *It's Only Rock 'n' Roll*. Keith and Mick decided that they would produce the album themselves under the name the Glimmer Twins. Keith's drug intake at this time was particularly bad and often astounded those around him. Music journalist Nick Evans recalls a particularly heavy session with Keith:

"He put a pile of heroin on the table that was easily half a gram and then he put down another of cocaine... I thought this was going to kill me, but I'm with Keith! Sniff! Oh Jesus Christ I was holding onto my chair but he was just getting started. This is what really frightened me. These drugs affected him physically in a very strange way... He'd taken an amount that you'd think would really do it and it wouldn't have any effect. He was staying up for nights and nights now, his engines were running but then... he'd fall asleep in mid-sentence for like a minute and then he'd wake up and continue the sentence. It was a bit disturbing because he was like living on this weird time."

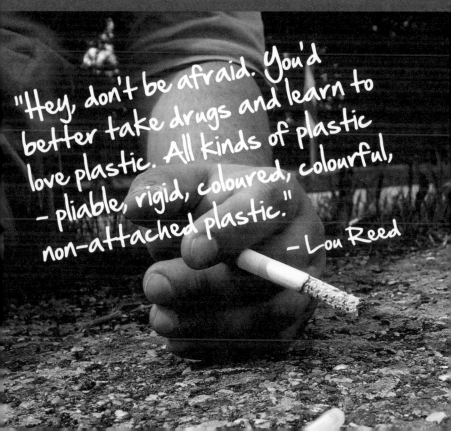

"Hey, don't be afraid. You'd better take drugs and learn to love plastic. All kinds of plastic – pliable, rigid, coloured, colourful, non-attached plastic."

– Lou Reed

1975 The Stones started to look for a new guitarist to replace Mick Taylor. They auditioned many major league guitarists but in the end settled on Ronnie Wood, lead guitarist for Rod Stewart's band, **The Faces**. One of the main criteria for selecting the new guitarist was that he should be insanely talented, a little unhinged and British. Ronnie ticked all the boxes plus a few more.

Their 1975 tour was remembered for the extravagant stage sets and lighting. Their tour manager wanted to include elephants but Keith put his foot down and refused: "Go on stage with a bloody elephant? Are you mad? I've paid my dues. I'm not working with no animal act. I worked with Elton and that was bad enough."

The Memphis Vice Squad threatened to arrest the band if they played their song *Starfucker*, the Stones' homage to the groupies that followed them around everywhere.

1976 Keith and Anita's son Tara died aged ten weeks. Keith insisted that the death was kept private and that they play their final Paris concert that night. He took the stage completely stoned and poured himself into the concert. His performance was so phenomenal that all the tracks on their album *Love You Live* were taken from that concert.

This probably marked a low point in Keith's life. He had just lost his son; offstage he was a barely functioning junkie and both mentally and physically he was close to a complete breakdown.

1977 Keith started the year by being found guilty of cocaine possession. A charge hanging over him from the previous year when he crashed his Bentley on the M1.

The band left the UK for a Canadian tour and Keith and Anita were arrested in Toronto. Keith was shooting up in the plane and the police later found the spoon he used to cook the heroin. He was so out of it when they came for him at the hotel that they had to slap him awake.

"WHAT DISAPPOINTED ME WAS THAT NONE OF THEM WAS WEARING A PROPER MOUNTIES UNIFORM WHEN THEY BURST INTO MY HOTEL ROOM. THEY WERE ALL IN ANORAKS WITH DROOPY MOUSTACHES AND BALD HEADS. REAL WEEDS, THE WHOLE LOT OF THEM, ALL JUST AFTER THEIR PICTURE IN THE PAPER. FIFTEEN OF 'EM ROUND MY BED, TRYING TO WAKE ME UP. I'D HAVE WOKEN UP A LOT QUICKER IF I'D SEEN THE RED TUNIC AND SMOKEY BEAR HAT."

1979 Keith released his first ever solo single featuring covers of *Run Rudolph Run* and *The Harder They Come*. He also formed a band called the **New Barbarians**, who played with him for his benefit concert for the blind in Canada.

"If you're going to kick authority in the teeth, you might as well use two feet."

— Keith

1980 Keith split up with Anita Pallenberg and later in the year met supermodel Patti Hansen. The couple were evicted from their New York apartment after complaints about their 24-hour rock 'n' roll lifestyle. Jagger's song *Neighbours* was written especially for Keith during this time. "I have a knack of finding a whole building of very cool people, you know, but there'll be one very uncool couple... *Neighbours* is the first song I think Mick's ever really written for me. It's one I wish I'd written."

Albert Goldman, the controversial author and critic, described Keith in the early 1980s:

"Look at his face. Keith has one of those great I've-done-it-all mugs you see in French movies of the Thirties... He does have a soul, he does look like what he is, and there's a very beautiful, delicate, tender and lyrical style that he has. ... Richards struck me as being, in some weird, almost mystical way... someone who gave himself up completely to the rock life. Who identified with it so completely, who did so little to protect himself from its dangers and traps, that he eventually developed a strange purity amidst the filth. He obtained a kind of blessedness in the gutter."

1982 Keith's home in Redlands is gutted by fire once again.

Patti Hansen had a positive influence on Keith's life and in 1982 encouraged Keith to get back in touch with his father, whom he hadn't spoken to in over 20 years. The two soon established a relationship based on their love of drinking. "All the things we couldn't stand about each other 20 years ago are all water under the bridge. In a way, he's giving me a lot of insight into why I'm like I am. Now we really appreciate each other."

Anita also commented on their likeness. "He's very narrow minded, very sheltered and shuttered and that helps to keep him going. He doesn't want to anything from outside... whether he's in Berlin or Tokyo, if you look in the fridge, there is always shepherd's pie. His father also only eats that kind of food. He won't do anything he doesn't want to do. I can see the resemblance, this kind of unmovable, unchangeable figure everybody flitters and moves around... And Keith flies off on tantrums and gets very threatening... Once a member of the crew ate his shepherd's pie and Keith threatened to cut him up and put his legs in a shepherd's pie."

"A kid once said to me 'Do you get hangovers?' I said, 'To get hangovers you have to stop drinking.'"

— Ian "Lemmy" Kilmister of Motorhead, 2006

Keith's Shepherd's Pie

3 lbs potatoes, peeled and diced
1 tablespoon butter
salt and pepper
2 large onions, chopped
2 lbs ground beef
2 large carrots, grated
2 (12 ounce) cans beef stock
1 tablespoon cornstarch or corn flour

- Place potatoes in a large saucepan.
- Cover with water and bring to a boil.
- Reduce heat, simmer until tender.
- Drain.
- Using an electric mixer or whisk, mash potatoes with butter.
- Season with salt and pepper and set aside.
- Heat a large skillet.
- Add beef and onions.
- Season with salt and pepper.
- Add carrots and stock.
- Mix in cornstarch and cook for 10 minutes.
- Pour into a pie dish and top with mashed potatoes.
- Place under grill until potatoes begin to turn brown.

1983 On 18 December, on his 40th birthday, Keith married Patti Hansen.

On falling out with Mick in the early '80s: **"IT'S NO FUN BEING AT LOGGERHEADS WITH ME. I CAN DRAIN THE ENERGY OUT OF ANYONE IF YOU'RE GOING TO FIGHT WITH ME. I DON'T ENJOY IT BUT I CAN BE A HARD FUCKER."**

Bill Flanagan, editor of *Musician* magazine, said in 1986: "Keith is rock's greatest contradiction, a monument of self-abuse who stays strong and vital year after year; a hard thick-skinned pirate who behaves like a perfect gentleman; the guru of hard rock and prototype for the image of the decadent rock star who writes melodic ballads in the tradition of Hoagy Carmichael."

1985 In 1985, Keith was asked to provide music for the Whoopi Goldberg comedy *Jumpin' Jack Flash*. He assembled an amazing all-star band which included Aretha Franklin on piano and lead vocals and Randy Jackson of *American Idol* fame on bass guitar.

In 1986, Patti gave birth to their first child, Alexandra Nicole. "Having babies roaming around your house is one of the most beautiful things in the world... It gives you that final missing link of what life's about. While they're looking upon you as the most wonderful person in the world because you're 'Daddy', they do more for you than you do for them."

"This is a very rootless life. The only thing you got to hang on to is family. I can sit at home with the kids and the wife and to me it's a perfectly rock 'n' roll natural wedding. My wife wakes me up and says 'Good Morning' to me, even though it may already be evening, then I go down to work..."

Patti Hansen & Keith

"Thank God Patti came into my life... On top of the fact I love the bitch to death, she keeps up with me, she keeps me going."

"I'm not the guys I see on MTV who obviously think they're me. There are so many people who think that's all there is to it. It's not that easy to be Keith Richards. But it's not so hard either. The main thing is to know yourself."

1986 Bill Wyman's affair with teenager Mandy Smith is exposed by the British tabloid press. In a somewhat perverse turn of events, his son later dated Mandy's mother, which presumably brings some sort of balance to the affair.

1988 Keith releases his first solo album *Talk Is Cheap*. His band, the **X-pensive Winos**, were named after Keith found them chugging a bottle of expensive wine at the back of the studio.

1989 By 1989, things had become so bad between Keith and Mick, and Keith was enjoying his new band so much that he decided to confront Mick and tell him it was all over for the Stones. They met in Barbados and Keith told Patti that the meeting might last 48 hours or two weeks depending on how things panned out. The meeting didn't start well with both of them screaming at each other in a furious row. However, pretty soon the mood changed and according to Keith they soon ended up laughing at the things they were supposed to have said about each other.

Keith: "We needed to clear the air, which, as old mates, we're very good at. Then, when we got into that room and sat down with our guitars, something entirely different took over. You can't define it, it's the same thing that always happens... The good thing is that once Mick and I actually sit down in a room to work, everything else goes out the window. On the third day I found myself unpacking. After four or five days Patti got through to me on the phone and said, 'Two weeks then?' I said, 'Happily, yes.'"

1990 A year after the fall of the Berlin Wall, Czech President Vaclav Havel invited The Rolling Stones to give a concert to celebrate their new freedom. The posters read: **"The Tanks are Rolling Out and The Stones are Rolling In."**

Keith: "That was an amazing gig. A ticket also acted as a one-day passport for fans coming from Poland, Hungary and Russia. A lot of the reason you've got major shifts in superpower situations in the past few years has to do with the past 20 years of music. You'll never get rid of nationalism... but the important thing is to spread the idea that there's really this one planet — that's really what we've got to worry about. And all these little lines that were drawn by guys hundreds of years ago are really obsolete. Music is the best communicator of all. In the long term, the most important thing that rock 'n' roll's done, it's opened up people's minds about these things. 'Cause you can't stop that shit. You can build a wall to stop people, but eventually the music, it'll cross that wall."

"ONE GOOD SONG IS WORTH A DOZEN ADDRESSES AND PROCLAMATIONS."
— JOE BARLOW, AMERICAN POET IN THE REVOLUTIONARY WAR

In fact, Havel proved himself an enlightened and open-minded leader by appointing Frank Zappa as Special Ambassador to the West on Trade, Culture and Tourism, much to the disgruntlement of US Secretary of State, James Baker, who famously declared: "You can do business with the United States or you can do business with Frank Zappa." Vaclav Havel still counts himself amongst Zappa's big fans, and says that "Frank Zappa was one of the gods of the Czech underground".

1991 The Stones signed a three-album deal with Richard Branson's **Virgin Records**. The advance on the deal was reportedly US$45 million.

In 1991, Ronnie Wood enhanced his reputation as the clown of the band by breaking his leg in a car crash then breaking the other leg while flagging down a car for help.

Two years later, in 1993, Bill Wyman announced that he was leaving the band.

1994 The Stones gain a reputation for being sharp businessmen. In 1994, they announced the launch of their own MasterCard and Visa credit cards and later in the year, their Dallas concert was the first concert ever to be broadcast over the Internet. The following year Microsoft announced that *Start Me Up* would be used as the theme music for the launch of their Windows 95 computer system.

1998 Ronnie Wood proves he's just as capable of courting death and disaster as Keith when a boat on which he's staying explodes off the Brazilian coast. He is rescued by the paparazzi — possibly the first time they have provided a useful service to the Stones. Not to be outdone, Keith falls off a ladder in his library a few weeks later, injuring his ribs and chest and causing the delay of the Stones' tour.

2006 While on holiday in Fiji, Keith suffered a mild concussion when he fell out of a coconut tree. A spokesman for Keith could not explain why the 62-year-old Keith was up a tree.

Keith stars as Captain Teague, Jack Sparrow's (Johnny Depp) father, in the film *Pirates of the Caribbean: At World's End*. Depp joins the long line of the rich and famous who fall under the spell of Keith and announces he will be making a film about Keith's life.

Captain
Teague Sparrow

2007 was also the year that music journal *NME* must have got on their knees and kissed the ground that Keith walks on for giving them the Exclusive of the Year. During an interview with the music magazine, Keith revealed: "The strangest thing I've tried to snort? My father. I snorted my father. He was cremated and I couldn't resist grinding him up with a little bit of blow. My dad wouldn't have cared, he didn't give a shit. It went down pretty well and I'm still alive."

In the same interview Keith talked about his own life expectancy: "I've no pretensions about immortality... I was number one on the Who's Likely To Die List for 10 years. I mean, I was really disappointed when I fell off the list."

 Hollywood director Martin Scorsese directs *Shine a Light*, a documentary film about the Stones' 2006 performance at the Beacon Theatre in New York. The movie showed backstage footage of the concert as well as clips from the Stones' early years. The film grossed over US$14 million at the box office.

2010 The Stones re-release a rarely seen movie of their 1972 concert, *Ladies and Gentlemen... the Rolling Stones*.

Keith Richards announces the release of his long-awaited autobiography, *Life*.

Find Yourself a Difficult Childhood

Placing yourself at the centre of a major global conflict may be a difficult thing to arrange but I think you'll find it's well worth the effort. The alternative is to adopt a broken family in a tough inner-city neighbourhood. Throw in an inspirational uncle with a cool name (it doesn't get much better than Theodore Augustus (Gus) Dupree) and easy access to drugs and your foot is firmly placed on the first rung of your career ladder to rock 'n' roll nirvana.

No Guns, No Glory

Develop whatever small semblance of talent you possess. Hell, you can train parrots to talk, dolphins to juggle and boy bands to lip-sync and dance in step, can it really be that difficult for you to become competent on just one instrument? If all else fails, play the drums. How hard can it be to hit something from point-blank range?

Music, mayhem and destruction have enjoyed a happy and passionate *ménage à trois* throughout the centuries. In the classic rock book *Hammer of the Gods: The Led Zeppelin Saga* by Stephen Davis, the author points out: "From time immemorial to well into the twentieth century, large armies went into battle accompanied by loud bands of martial drums and trumpets... As the music blared, bearers passed through the army with rations of wine or other intoxicants so that the warriors, in their late teens and early twenties, could fortify and encourage themselves into a furious, fear-deadened lust for blood and slaughter. As the troops, now dazed and confused, began to charge, the music was played even louder, faster. Bands of opposing armies had to compete against each other as well. Sometimes the best band won the day. The drum major was an important part of the battle, setting the pace of the action. The trumpets became efficient signals above the horrid, confusing, loud din of battle; even today bugle calls survive in modern armed forces, the last vestiges of the dreaded din, the cries of dying men, the clash of horses and spears, the echoes of bronze, of steel, of canon.

Substitute the electric guitar for the trumpet. Add Robert's whispered tales of glory, of old battles and bloodlust, plus Bonzo's steady cannonade. Add 10,000 rock fans dazed and confused by grass, cheap wine, and the new soporific of choice, Quaalade (Mandrax in Europe). With their epic explosions of sound and light, Led Zeppelin seemed to be a sublimation for the din of battle, a wargasm experience for its audience. It was no accident that the young American troops in Vietnam took Led Zeppelin to heart."

Davis' description of Led Zeppelin's wargasmic experience could equally well have been written about the Stones in the same era. The chaos and anarchy that followed the Stones around was not confined to their screaming fans. The constant conflict between the various members of the band over the years has led to many moments of tension, but has also produced moments of sublime beauty.

From the earliest days of the Stones, the tensions between the various band members, but especially between Mick, Keith and Brian Jones, resulted in a bizarre creative edge:

> **"IT MADE THEM EVEN MORE HOSTILE AND ARROGANT, FRAGMENTED THEIR MUSIC, AND CREATED AN IMAGE OF REJECTION THAT WOULD REPRESENT A DEFINITIVE DEPARTURE FROM ANYTHING THAT HAD GONE BEFORE THEM IN BRITISH CULTURE."**
>
> **– VICTOR BOCKRIS**

What is extraordinary is that the core of the Stones has stayed more or less intact since the early '60s. Sure, dozens of supporting musicians have come and gone but Mick, Keith and Charlie keep rolling, along with Ronnie, who is still the 'new boy' since his debut in 1975. The band is like a multinational corporation with the boys as directors and a stream of class musicians and support staff trailing in their wake. However, to torture the corporate metaphor a little further, the Stones are less like The Body Shop than Exxon. These guys are completely ruthless when it comes to business.

The entire history of the Stones consists of them taking people into their group and then spitting them out when they were no longer of use. Johnny Phelge, Alexis Korner, Giorgio Gromelsky, Andrew Oldham, Brian Jones, Ian Stewart... even Bill Wyman wistfully remarked:

"THEY DIDN'T LIKE ME BUT I HAD A GOOD AMPLIFIER AND THEY WERE BADLY IN NEED OF AMPLIFIERS AT THAT TIME."

Luckily for Bill, he managed to hang in there even when they could afford decent amps.

As well as being a tough businessman, Keith also has a reputation for being a bit of a hard man, one not afraid to fight his corner when the going gets tough. After returning from their first US tour in 1964, the Stones were playing in Blackpool when a Glaswegian gang started to cause trouble. After fighting their way to the front of the stage they started to spit on the band. Keith, never backward in coming forward, strode to the front of the stage, smashed his heel into the hand of the gang leader then kicked him full in the face. The Stones then fled the stage before the gang could get their revenge.

> "The Stones were the first to say 'Up against the wall Motherfucker' and they said it with class."
>
> — US critic Jim Landau

A few months earlier on the US tour, Keith had nearly died when an electric fault with his guitar caused an explosion that flung him across the stage. "My guitar touched the microphone stand and my mouth hit the microphone and all I saw was a flash and some smoke. I woke up an hour later in Sacramento General Hospital with a doctor saying, 'They either come around or they don't.'"

Perhaps the most heartless episode in the history of the Stones was their treatment of Brian Jones. The man who helped found the band and one of the main reasons for their success was chucked out unceremoniously when he ceased to be of any use to them.

One study revealed that of the 700 most popular songs of "heavy metal", 50% speak of killings, 35% of Satanism and 7% about suicide. Sheila Davis, professor of lyric writing at New York University, is convinced that society should "give serious attention to the content of pop songs and to evaluate not only what lyrics are saying to society but, more important, what they may be doing to it."

— USA Today, October 11, 1985

Keith: "I wasn't surprised about Brian. I didn't wish him dead and there were a few guys who did, but in all honesty it was no surprise. And it was hard to shed a tear at his demise... It was like 'Wow, he's gone, thank God.' Cold-blooded as that sounds, he was a passenger for us. We had to cover his ass. We all revere his memory and nobody deserves to go that young. But if anybody asked for it, he did... **YOU DON'T LEAVE THE STONES SINGING, YOU JUST GET CARRIED OUT."**

Keith's entire journey with the Stones has been one long battle — with Mick, drugs, the police, Anita Pallenberg, drugs, the courts, alcohol, fellow musicians, drugs...

In 1972, Keith and Anita went to Jamaica where reggae was beginning to take off. Soon after arriving Keith bought Tommy Steele's house, **Point of View**, a beautiful property overlooking Cutlass Bay. The neighbours must have wondered what the hell had happened. From cheerful, chirpy vaudeville entertainer Tommy Steele to... Keith.

Keith used the house as his private getaway when not touring and with drugs freely available in the earthly paradise of Jamaica, Keith regularly found himself in a very bad state.

After their tour of the East in 1973, Keith returned to Jamaica to find that Anita had surrounded herself with a tough bunch of locals with whom she was clearly very intimate. He was warned by members of the local white community that her behaviour wouldn't be tolerated and that he had to do something about it. Humiliated, Keith fled the island, leaving Anita and the kids with the local guys.

Soon after he left Jamaica, the house was raided and Anita was arrested for possession of marijuana. She was thrown into a local prison cell where she was allegedly abused by both prisoners and guards. It took a major effort from Keith to have her released and flown to the UK. In retrospect, it's astonishing that both Keith and Anita survived their relationship with each other at all. Both seemed to feed off each other's destructive nature to create a continuous stream of drama and disaster.

However, Keith managed to provide enough drama of his own, even when Anita wasn't around. In 1978, he had another close shave while staying at a friend's house in the US.

"There was a big party one night and somebody had turned the gas fire off — but not all the way. So the gas was still going and there was some incense burning and then there was a spark... Boom! I'm in the bedroom with... my girlfriend of the hour. I wake up and the room's full of smoke and she's crashed out and I sniff. I open the door to the bedroom and **I'M LOOKING AT A FIREBALL RUSHING DOWN THE CORRIDOR TOWARDS THE OXYGEN... AND ME!"**

"At our best,
we master the art of
going just over the edge
of the abyss,
then pulling back."

"... There's the two of us, stark naked. Half the house is destroyed, the roof is falling in on us but we've managed to get through — with a few burns here and there — to the swimming pool. Stark fucking bullock naked with this blonde, bless 'er heart, good girl, solid gold, saying to me, 'Do something!' And I said, 'What do you want me to do, piss on it?!' The weird thing is this house burned down totally, except for one wooden stump of a pillar and in the bedroom this little portion of a chest of drawers which had like my passport, all my favourite tapes, jewellery, a shooter with 500 rounds of ammunition. All untouched. And a friend of went back the next day when everything else was still too hot to touch, smouldering, and came back with all my stuff."

Ah, the charmed life of Mr Richards.

"The things that would kill other people don't kill me. Despite everything, I'm a survivor. I can only suppose that I possess the kind of mentality and psychological make-up that could handle it. I come from very tough stock."

— Keith, in an interview with Stanley Booth, 1989

"IT IS REPORTED THAT CURRENTLY THERE ARE: 13 ROCK GROUPS NAMED AFTER MALE SEXUAL ORGANS, SIX NAMED AFTER FEMALE SEXUAL ORGANS, FOUR NAMED BY VARIATIONS OF THE WORD 'SPERM', EIGHT NAMED WITH WORDS LINKED WITH ABORTION, ONE NAMED AFTER A DISEASE OF THE WOMB. THERE ARE ADDITIONALLY 10 GROUPS NAMED IN HONOR OF VARIOUS SEXUAL ACTS WHILE THE NAMES OF EIGHT GROUPS INCLUDE SWEAR WORDS AGAINST MOTHERS."

— US NEWS AND WORLD REPORT, MARCH 19, 1990

On the *"Tattoo You"* tour in 1981, Keith gave Ronnie Woods a very hard time about his drug habit — somewhat ironic considering his own jet-fuelled past. Things eventually came to a head one night, as Woods recalled: "He'd been up for days and he thought that I'd been cheating on my wife and doing dope and suddenly there was this madman leading a posse of my wife, his wife, a huge string of people. God, when we collided! *Boom!* He got the first one in — hit me in the nose — and I got up and smacked him. It was all over in 10 minutes and it actually cleared the air. We got very close after that. I was covered in blood and walked into the next room, where Mick and Charlie were working and I said, "What do you think of this?" and Mick said,

"HOW DOES THE MIDDLE EIGHT OF *SUMMER ROMANCE* GO?"

On the last night of the tour, a fan eluded security and ran on the stage. Keith belted him on the head with his guitar and carried on playing. Ronnie said, "Hey Keith, he's only a fan. No reason to fuckin' hit him." And Keith replied, "Oh yeah. What if he had a fucking gun in his hand or knife? I mean he might be a fan. He might be a nutter, and he's on my turf. I'm gonna chop the mother down!"

While most of us would run a mile to avoid life's agonies, Keith seems to enjoy confronting them and poking them in the eye. In a *Rolling Stones* interview in 2002, Keith was asked if he had a fear of anything at all.

"My reaction is to get ice cold. And that makes me mad. I have to worry about this. This red curtain comes down, and then I'm liable to do anything. But fear? As a kid, I knew it real well. I'm this little squirt, and every day when I go home from school, no matter which route I take, I'm gonna get beat up. It was around then that I banished it... fear. I learned how to take a beating and how to get a good one in now and again. It taught me to toughen myself up."

"I'VE SEEN MURDERS. I'VE SEEN DOGS COME ON STAGE TRYING TO SAVAGE PEOPLE. I'VE TURNED ROUND AND FOUND A POOL OF BLOOD WHERE THE PIANO PLAYER SHOULD BE! I'VE BEEN STRUCK BY SHARPENED PENNIES. BUT YOU CAN'T REALLY DO ANYTHING ABOUT THAT. IT'S JUST A PART OF THE GIG."

– KEITH ON TOURING

The tough kid from Dartford has gone further than most of the local tough guys and at the same time, established a reputation as being a bit of a philosopher.

"TO ME, THE MAIN THING
ABOUT LIVING ON THIS
PLANET IS TO KNOW WHO
THE HELL YOU ARE AND TO
BE REAL ABOUT IT. THAT'S
THE REASON I'M STILL
ALIVE... I'VE LIVED MY LIFE
MY OWN WAY, AND I'M HERE
BECAUSE I'VE TAKEN THE
TROUBLE TO FIND OUT
WHO I AM."

— KEITH

If you wanna be wild, you gotta be tough and ruthless. Monsters of rock 'n' roll are not sensitive tree huggers (Bono you can leave the room...). They are the bodysurfers of life, hurling themselves into the maelstrom. Occasionally the crowd is going to part and you're going to end up face down in a pool of your own blood feeling slightly foolish. Do you care? Do you hell! You are a Wild Man. You are the Beast of Rock 'n' Roll! You da Tough Guy! You just get right back on that stage and hurl yourself out there again. The pain is never as bad the second time around.

Make friends and influence people... then kick them out and find better, more interesting, more well-connected and useful friends. Imagine you are the CEO of a large multinational with employees who have served you faithfully for 25 years. You shake their hand, give them a speech and a weekend in Miami with the family. You know they have been coasting for the last ten years but what the hell — loyalty must be rewarded.

HOW TO BE WILD

Now imagine you are the CEO of the wildest band in the world. Do you reward 25 years of service? I don't think so. If anyone lasts longer than five years you really have to question whether they are fully embracing the corporate ethic — or lack of it. Never mind why are they still with us after five years — why aren't they in rehab like the rest of us? Why aren't they dead? The only two guys to ride out the Rolling Stones storm for any length of time are Prince Loewenstein and Ian Stewart. One is an accountant and the other was their tour manager. OK, so somebody needs to stay sober and put the children to bed. Just make sure it isn't you.

They claim that music hath charms to soothe the savage beast. But what if the beast is lurking in the rhythm section? One of the earliest musicians to enjoy a fiendish reputation was not, as you might expect, one of the Blues boys from the Mississippi Delta, but Italian **Niccolo Paganini** (1782—1840). It's hard to believe but the eminent classical violinist has a lot in common with Keith. For a start they actually look alike — especially when Keith was in his cadaverous phase in the early 1970s; they both changed the tuning of their instruments to alter their musical sound; they were both wild haired men with a reputation for a debauched lifestyle — Paganini was a drinks, gambling and women kind of a guy, very much like Keith; and finally, they both had a reputation for having done a deal with the Devil.

Paganini was an exceptional violinist and composer who was disfigured by disease and genetic mutation into a freakish violin-playing genius. He actually suffered from two rare diseases — **Ehlers-Danlos** — which allowed him remarkable joint mobility in his fingers, and **Marfan Syndrome** — which gave him long limbs and fingers. This combination allowed him to develop certain techniques which are virtually impossible to imitate, even by the greatest of violinists.

Unlike his predecessors, he did not stand still and play in a conservative upright manner but threw himself into a frenzy when playing. It was reported that at some of his performances women would faint at the sight of the whirling figure and at one famous concert, the audience even claimed to have seen the Devil guiding his hands.

Paganini loved his reputation as the Devil's bad boy and played up to it wherever he went. He enhanced his pale, cadaverous features by always wearing black. One commentator described his "pale, long-drawn face with its hollow cheeks, his thin lips that seemed to curl into a sardonic smile, [and the] piercing expression of his eyes which were like flaming charcoals, [that] gave him a diabolic appearance..."

Sound like anyone you know?

One of Keith's earliest musical influences was US blues legend Robert Johnson. An outstanding guitarist, Johnson cited his main musical influence as being the Devil. That's right, ol' Beelzebub himself. According to Johnson he came face to face with the Brimstone Breather at a crossroads in Mississippi and sold his soul to him in return for his musical talents. Johnson wrote a number of devilishly inspired songs, including *Crossroad Blues, Preaching Blues (Up Jumped the Devil)*, *Hellhound On My Trail* and *Me and the Devil Blues*. Johnson died under mysterious circumstances in 1938, supposedly poisoned by the husband of one of his many girlfriends.

Maybe taking a leaf out of Johnson's playbook, the Stones also went through a spell in the late 1960s when they were alleged to be dabbling in the occult. In his book, *The Ultimate Evil*, investigator-author Maury Terry writes that between 1966 and 1967, a Satanic cult called the Process Church "sought to recruit the Rolling Stones and the Beatles". During this period, Terry reports that a photo of Mick Jagger's longtime girlfriend, Marianne Faithfull, appeared in an issue of *The Process Magazine*. The picture shows her lying, as if dead, clutching a rose.

A key link between the Rolling Stones and the Process Church was Kenneth Anger, a follower of Aleister Crowley, the founder of modern Satanism (a man once described as " the most evil man in Britain"). Anger, who was born in 1930, and was a child Hollywood movie star, became a devoted disciple of Crowley. Anger himself admits that he did attempt to get the Stones involved in the occult: "The active magical element in the Stones' music is its strong sexual connotations. It's basically music to fuck to. I was going to film a version of *Lucifer Rising* with the Stones. All the roles were to be carefully cast, with Mick being Lucifer and Keith as Beelzebub..."

However that didn't happen in the end. Anger, commenting on Anita, said, "I believe that Anita is, for want of a better word, a witch... The occult unit within the Stones was Keith and Anita... and Brian. You see, Brian was a witch too."

Aleister Crowley

Keith denies he was ever that much into Satanism but Tony Sanchez, the group's constant companion, claims that he once found satanic paraphernalia in Anita's room. The rumours were no doubt flamed by the release of the Stones' album *Their Satanic Majesties* in 1967. This was followed the following year by *Beggar's Banquet*, featuring the single *Sympathy for the Devil*. In a TV special called *Rock and Roll Circus*, the Stones perform the song and Jagger takes off his shirt to reveal portraits of the Devil on his arms and chest.

Keith in 2002: "*Sympathy* is quite an uplifting song. It's just a matter of looking the Devil in the face. He's there all the time. I've had very close contact with Lucifer — I've met him several times. Evil — people tend to bury it and hope it sorts itself out and doesn't rear its ugly head. *Sympathy for the Devil* is just as appropriate now, with 9/11. There it is again, big time. When that song was written, it was a time of turmoil. It was the first sort of international chaos since World War II. And confusion is not the ally of peace and love. You want to think the world is perfect. Everybody gets sucked into that. And as America has found out to its dismay, you can't hide. You might as well accept the fact that evil is there and deal with it any way you can. *Sympathy for the Devil* is a song that says:

'DON'T FORGET HIM'. IF YOU CONFRONT HIM, THEN HE'S OUT OF A JOB."

Jimi Hendrix, another guitar great from the 1960s, also admitted to occult influences. His former girlfriend, Fayne Pridgon, said: "He used to always talk about some devil or something was in him, you know, and he didn't have any control over it, he didn't know what made him act the way he acted and what made him say the things he said, and songs... just came out of him."

The Stones have also been accused of backmasking, or inserting reverse, subliminal messages into their albums, along with other bands. The practice of recording a message, playing it backwards then inserting it into a song began with the Beatles' album *Revolver* in 1966. The song *Revolution 9* allegedly includes the reversed message "Paul is a dead man, miss him, miss him, miss him". This would have been freaky if Paul had died but he and Ringo are the longest living of the Beatles. Other evil bands that have incorporated subliminal messages in their songs include Slayer, Judas Priest, Led Zeppelin, ELO, Pink Floyd and Queen.

> They'd say "if you play the record backwards, you can hear evil things like grrrr!" and I would think, "Jeez, I didn't know the devil sounded like that. I thought he was coherent, like the rest of us.
>
> — Brian Johnson of AC/DC, 2001

While it's easy to laugh off such gimmicks as the work of an over-creative, or even drug-sated mind, there are those who will always take matters just a little too far. Such groups include some of the Scandinavian Black Metal groups. These anti-religious, anarchic groups have their origins in heavy metal and punk and have been accused of burning down churches and satanic worship. Readers may think that the rivalry between the Beatles and the Rolling Stones was intense, or maybe feel that Oasis and Pulp overstepped the mark with their backstage punch-ups... however, this all pales in comparison to rivals in the Norwegian Black Metal scene. Perhaps the most extreme example of this concerns the band Mayhem and the death of their lead singer, Dead.

Dead was a Swede who joined Mayhem when his band Morbid folded in 1988. As a child he had suffered a near-death experience that convinced him that he had died and was now a being from another world. His beliefs are reflected in the vampiric lyrics he wrote for *De Mysteriis Dom Sathanas*.

Interestingly, the dark lyrics to this particular song segue rather nicely with a story about **KISS**, although it does seem somewhat lame and insipid in comparison to folk tales from their Scandinavian cousins.

In a bizarre way that can only be achieved by men who wear a lot of make-up and leather, the members of KISS also liked to push the boundaries of good taste. But not via anarchy, Satanism and church burning. Their contribution was more in line with services to the printing industry that would have made Johannes Gutenberg proud. In 1977, KISS decided that to promote themselves to people with learning difficulties (surely their largest target market), they would publish *KISS: The Comic*. Obviously sensitive to the fact that having their own comic might not be seen as radical enough in the rock 'n' roll community, they decided to spice it up a bit. Thus in February 1977 band members Gene Simmons, Ace Frehley, Paul Stanley and Peter Criss all gave blood to be mixed in with the printer's ink for the first edition of the comic.

The story ends on a bit of a sad note though. It was rumoured that due to a mix-up at the printers, the batch of blood red ink was actually used on an edition of *Sports Illustrated* instead of the KISS comic.

Anyway, I digress. Back to Dead and his unhealthy obsession with the Netherworld (as opposed to most musicians who are usually more obsessed with their nether regions... but more of Bill Wyman later). Dead reputedly carried around the rotting body of a crow in a jar and would inhale its fumes before taking the stage so he could perform with the stench of death in his nostrils. He also took to donning a white greasepaint visage to impersonate dead bodies. "It wasn't anything to do with the way KISS and Alice Cooper used make-up," says Necro Butcher, the bass player. "Dead actually wanted to look like a corpse. He didn't do it to look cool. He would draw snot dripping out of his nose. That doesn't look cool. He called it corpse-paint."

When Dead first arrived in Norway, Necro Butcher took it upon himself to make sure their new singer had somewhere to live and was looked after. However, the lead guitarist and founder of the band — Euronymous — did his best to make him feel uncomfortable. "He tried to psych him out," says Necro Butcher. "He would tell Dead, 'We don't like you. You should just kill yourself.' Stuff like that."

And then, one day in the spring of 1991, Dead surprised everyone and did just that. Euronymous came back to their house to discover his body slumped against a wall.

"Rock has always been devil's music."
— David Bowie

He had slashed his wrists with a butcher's knife and blown his brains out with a shotgun. Managing to maintain a perverse sense of humour even on the brink of death, his suicide note read: "Excuse all the blood. Let the party begin."

Euronymous, who discovered the body, proceeded to take pictures of Dead's remains before notifying the police. Necro Butcher acknowledged that the scandal was excellent for publicity but there was a downside: "Every time we lost a member we had to find somebody else to replace them and start the whole rehearsing process again. We suffered in that way as a band." Well you would, wouldn't you?

Unfortunately for Euronymous, the death of Dead led to the introduction of Varg Vikernes, also known as Count Grishnackh, as the new guitarist. Euronymous decided that he would inflict the same mind games on Varg as he had with Dead and threatened to send some people over to torture him to death. While this was probably just Euronymous' way of passing the long winter evenings in Norway, the threats were taken as real by Varg who decided to get his retaliation in first. On 10 August

Euronymous

1993, an unsuspecting Euronymous opened the door to Vikernes, who burst into his apartment and stabbed him 24 times in the chest, back and head. Vikernes and his accomplice, Snorre Ruch (fellow guitarist), were sentenced to 21 years in jail.

I ask you, how much good publicity can one band handle?

"THE ONLY NEGATIVE THING ABOUT MURDER IS THAT WHEN YOU KILL SOMEONE THEY CAN NO LONGER SUFFER."
– VARG VIKERNES OF MAYHEM, 1993

Other bands that claim to have been inspired by the Devil and his disciples include Led Zeppelin. The founder of Led Zeppelin, Jimmy Page, owned an occult bookstore in London for many years and was a keen supporter of the notorious occultist Alisteir Crowley. In 1978 he said of Crowley:

"I feel Aleister Crowley is a misunderstood genius of the twentieth century. Because his whole thing was liberation of the person, of the entity, and that restrictions would foul you up, lead to frustration which leads to violence, crime, mental breakdown, depending on what sort of makeup you have underneath. The further this age we're in now gets into technology and alienation, a lot of the points he's made seem to manifest themselves all down the line."

A famous Los Angeles groupie from the 1970s, Miss Pamela, described how Jimmy was really into whips and S&M and the occult: "I believe that Jimmy was very into black magic and probably did a lot of rituals, candles, bat's blood, the whole thing... And, of course, the rumour that I've heard forever is that they all made this pact with the Devil, Satan, for Black Power, whatever, so that Zeppelin would be such a huge success. And the only one that didn't do it was John Paul Jones. He wouldn't do it. Who knows where the rumour came from? But that was the rumour."

Page even went so far as to buy Crowley's former mansion, Boleskine House, on the shores of Loch Ness. Zeppelin's drummer, John Bonham, died in the house in 1980. It's alleged that Robert Plant split the group up after his death and blamed Page's obsession with the occult for his death.

So there you have it. Rock 'n' roll is in fact the Devil's music and can have a seriously detrimental effect on your spiritual development. Billy Graham was right all along. To confirm our suspicions, a woman named Dorothy Retallack published a book called *The Sound of Music and Plants*. Ms Retallack conducted experiments on plants at the Colorado Woman's College in Denver using the school's Biotronic Control Chambers. She placed plants in a chamber and played various kinds of music to each plant. We are told that "she was astounded at what she discovered".

When relaxing, 'middle-of-the-road' music was played to the plants they grew strong and bushy and leaned towards the speaker. When played a special mix of Jimi Hendrix, Vanilla Fudge, and Led Zeppelin, the result was "chaos, pure chaos" with plants showing a variety of ailments, including small leaves and gangly or stunted growth.

It was recorded that the plants showed absolutely no response to Country & Western music.

Sell your Soul to Rock `n` Roll!

1. Find a deserted and distant crossroads and wait for a moonless night.

2. Loiter around the crossroads at midnight strumming or scratching your instrument of choice.

3. Await the arrival of a dark and swarthy gentleman with a curious bulge in the back of his pants and startling deformity on forehead, wearing brimstone-based cologne.

4. When aforementioned gentleman offers to tune your instrument as down-payment for future option on your soul and a lifetime of wealth, fame and fortune, accept with much enthusiasm and shake the man by the hand.

5. Your hand will probably continue to shake for the rest of your life, but the rewards will be generous.

6. Live for the moment. Don't think too much about your fiery future.

For most bands, the ultimate achievement in their career is a number one single. A select few may achieve their aim, burn brightly for a few years and then die a slow and painful death. **The Rolling Stones** are one of only a handful of bands that move in a different stratosphere to the rest. They have been around for almost 50 years and can still pack stadiums wherever they play. In 2006, they played a free concert on Brazil's Copacabana Beach and drew an audience of over a million people. Did I say it was free? The show was advertised as free, but actually the City of Rio paid US$750,000 for the event. Thank you, taxpayers!

Truth of the matter is, you don't get to hang around for long in the music industry unless you develop a thick skin and a long, deep streak of nastiness. The Stones may look like a bunch of laidback, easygoing, fun guys but beating within their collective body is a business heart and brain as cunning as that of Donald Trump... if indeed the Donald does actually possess a heart. In business and life they have become shrewd and sharp, having learned a few tough lessons along the way.

"You had to be tough to be in the Stones," said Bill Wyman in his autobiography *Stoned Alone*. He wasn't kidding. The fall-out rate surrounding the Stones is on a par with an SAS selection course.

Keith himself commented: "The Rolling Stones destroy people at an alarming rate. Something about us makes us come face to face eventually with themselves, sometimes for the better, sometimes in the worst possible way. Maybe that ultimately is the most important thing about the Stones. For some unknown reason they strike at a person at a point and in a position that they don't even know exists."

The Stones' first manager (albeit on a very informal basis) was Georgio Gomelsky, a Russian immigrant. George can legitimately claim to have been one of the founders of BRB (British Rhythm and Blues), a phrase he coined as a journalist at *Jazz News*. George gave the Stones their first break by booking them to play their first gig at the Station Hotel in Richmond. Only three people turned up for their first concert, not helped by heavy snowfall and George's advertising billboard outside, which advertised the event as a "Rhythm and Bulls" concert.

Slowly, week by week, the audience grew. Many of the audience came from local art colleges and included musicians such as Eric Clapton, who turned up clutching some rare Blues albums and would sometimes act as a DJ between sets. George recalled:

"Slowly, a pattern for the evening emerged. The first set was a kind of warm-up; new songs and arrangements were tried out, almost like a public rehearsal. Then there was a 45 minute break and everyone went to the bar to partake in a jar or two. Since we had to be out of the place by 10 pm, the second set would start around 9:15. By now everyone was tanked-up and the music more intense."

Eventually, the Crawdaddy Club became so popular it had to move to a larger venue at the nearby Richmond Athletic Association. The club didn't produce many great athletes but it did produce great acts such as the Stones and the Yardbirds. Looking back on that time, Georgio sees it as the beginning of a major movement in British music.

"You hear about
bands who say,
'We did one show
where only 20 people
showed up', well that
was our average gig
for five years."

— Dexter Holland of
    The Offspring, 1995

"Forty years later, what does it look like? There is something beyond scale in the unprecedented length and perspicacity of the Stones' career." (George's English has also improved over the years.) "There's also an enigmatic, slippery yet fateful part; sometimes success can set you apart from the rest of humanity. Attempting to make total sense of it is like holding sand in one's hand or watching a train hurtle past you in the night."

While playing at the Crawdaddy Club, the Stones were approached by the 19-year-old **Andrew Loog Oldham**, who offered to be their publicist. The remarkably precocious Oldham had already worked with Brain Epstein and the Beatles and was keen to take on the Stones as well.

Keith: "Andrew pulled together the innate talents within the band. He turned us into a gang, in a way, a sort of conspiracy. And he broadened our horizons. Our biggest aim at the time was to be the best blues band in London and that would have done it for us. But Andrew said 'What are you talking about? Look, I've just come from working with these four berks from Liverpool. You can easily do this.' He had the experience — even though he was just as young as we were — but he was also very precocious: a sharp fucker and a right little gangster. Also he really wanted to be one of the band. At one time he called himself 'the sixth Rolling Stone', so as well as the management side, he thought of himself as part of the gang."

It was Oldham who realised in 1964 that the Stones' profile could be raised considerably by becoming the anti-Beatles. John, Paul, George and Ringo always looked cool and enjoyed broad-based appeal. Oldham encouraged the

Stones to wear their hair long and their clothes loud and they soon stirred up British society with their wild antics. Oldham came up with the slogan **"Would You Let Your Daughter Go Out with a Rolling Stone?"**. This cunning strategy has been repeated ad nauseum by just about every manager and publicist in the music industry ever since, culminating perhaps most successfully in Malcolm MacLaren and the Sex Pistols in 1975.

"BACK THEN, YOU WERE DEALING WITH MAGIC. NOW YOU ARE DEALING WITH THE REALITY OF BEAN COUNTING. THE STONES AND I GAVE EACH OTHER CONFIDENCE. A LOT OF IT HAD TO DO WITH BEING THE SAME AGE, SAME LACK OF EXPERIENCE AND SAME PASSION FOR LIFE. IN MANY WAYS, I MANAGED THEM LESS THAN I INSPIRED THEM TO BECOME WHAT THEY BECAME."

– ANDREW OLDHAM

Like all bands, there were people who would try and rip them off along the way. When Robert Stigwood, a music promoter, allegedly refused to pay them royalties for an Australian tour, he was confronted by Keith at a London club. A music journalist Keith Altham describes how Keith "started to kick the shit out of him. Every time Stigwood tried to get up, Keith would belt him again. 'Keith', I said 'why do you keep hitting him?' ... 'Because he keeps getting up', he replied."

Oldham spent three years building up the band and in that time achieved two major accomplishments with the Stones. The first was to lock Keith and Mick in a room and tell them not to come out until they had written a song. This was the beginning of the Jagger/Richards songwriting partnership that, in many ways, became just as successful as Lennon and McCartney.

His second achievement was to secure them a record deal with Decca records.

Keith: "Andrew got the deal at Decca Records — like lightning. The beautiful thing was that Dick Rowe at Decca had turned down the Beatles. Was he going to say 'no' twice? So we knew we had them over a barrel before we even started negotiating, which is why we could do it the way we did it, having artistic control, recording for our own company, and leasing Decca our tracks, so that when we were recording we didn't have a little bloke in a brown coat coming round and telling us 'I think there should be more violins on it'."

"... I didn't realise quite what an amazing fissure that put into the establishment, because those monolithic empires, EMI or Decca, were just like the British Empire or the Bank of England to me. But Andrew educated us really quickly that the people who were running these institutions had no idea what was happening, that they'd really lost touch..."

I hate to say it, but we were Nazi-like in our brutal attack on Decca."

Eventually, the Stones tired of Oldham, who became a liability due to his drug and alcohol excesses. Besides that he had also just become too weird to represent them. In 1965, a tough, unscrupulous New York operator named Allen Klein took over from Oldham. We have already looked at how the Stones dabbled in Satanism in the late '60s. The more you learn about Klein, the more you wonder if he wasn't a direct appointment from the Devil himself. Most people who worked with him proclaimed him to be the original fork-tongued serpent.

The Stones didn't even appoint Klein directly. Oldham sold his share to Klein without asking permission from the Stones. Klein was to give the Stones their toughest lesson in business. His business philosophy was best summed up by the sign on his desk that read: **"YEA THOUGH I WALK THROUGH THE VALLEY OF THE SHADOW OF DEATH I SHALL FEAR NO EVIL, FOR I AM THE BIGGEST BASTARD IN THE VALLEY."**

Klein successfully negotiated the Stones' first million-dollar contract. However, he gained notoriety for what happened after he was fired by the Stones in 1970. Klein's company ABKCO successfully sued the Stones for sacking him and as part of the settlement, retained the rights to all the Stones' songs from 1963 to 1969. Despite legal action, the Stones have never been able to wrestle the rights to their own songs back from Klein. Keith describes the settlement as "the price of an education".

"I THINK RECORD COMPANIES ARE CRIMINALS."

– JON BON JOVI, 2001

Just about every story concerning Klein involves quite astonishing duplicity. During the filming of the Stones' rock 'video' *Rock and Roll Circus*, Klein met John Lennon. The Beatles' manager Brian Epstein had recently passed away. It took two years but Lennon convinced Ringo Starr and George Harrison that Klein should take over the business of The Beatles. Paul McCartney didn't want him and refused to sign the agreement. The discord this created among the group was one of the main contributing factors in the break-up of The Beatles.

Years later, Klein screwed over George Harrison. While Klein was acting as business manager for George Harrison, the former Beatle was sued for using the melody of *He's So Fine* in his hit single *My Sweet Lord*. Klein went out and bought the rights to the earlier song, but continued to fight George's claim behind his back, knowing that either way he would win.

George Harrison: "He, on one hand, was defending me, then he switched sides and continued the lawsuit. And every time the judge said what the result was, he'd appeal. And he kept appealing and appealing until it got to the Supreme Court... this thing went on for 16 years or something... 18 years. And finally, it's all over with, and the result of it is I own *My Sweet Lord*, and I now own *He's So Fine*, and Allan Klein owes me like three or four hundred thousand dollars 'cause he took all the money on both songs. It's really a joke. It's a total joke."

The Stones' business dealings were taken over in 1970 by **Prince Rupert Ludwig Ferdinand zu Leowenstein-Wertheim-Freudenberg**, or Roopy to his mates (nah, I just made that bit up). For a band that prided itself on being so anti-establishment, the appointment of Rupert Loewenstein was something of a shock. However, he has remained the Stones' financial manager ever since and proved to be a rock of stability for the band. If the Stones had difficulties with the appointment, imagine the difficulties faced by Loewenstein when selling the potential new clients to his partners.

Said Loewenstein: "Of course the lifestyle of such a band was different from that of the chief executives of, say, ICI or British Aluminium, though the human problems encountered were not all that dissimilar. Even, we gather, politicians can have complicated emotional relationships and gullibility and over-enthusiasms are not unknown even in the most elevated corporate circles. However, it was hard at that time to convince City bankers and solicitors of this, and indeed the much-publicised antics of rock stars did l ittle to help when the Rolling Stones' early contracts had to be interpreted by a series of judges."

Although the financial and business side of the Stones was now sorted, they would face numerous other problems as the years went by. The biggest of these problems was the fall-out rate of colleagues and fellow musicians due to deaths from drugs and drink.

Brian Jones was the first to go in 1969, destroyed by years of drug abuse.

In September 1973, Gram Parsons died of an overdose at the Joshua Tree Inn in California. **"PEOPLE WERE DROPPING LIKE FLIES THEN. IT WAS NOTHING TO WAKE UP ONCE A WEEK AND HEAR SO-AND-SO'S GONE…NOBODY SEEMED TO DIE OF ANYTHING BUT ODs IN THOSE DAYS."**

– KEITH

Two weeks after Gram Parsons died, Bobby Keys, one the Stones' regular saxophonists and tour musicians, collapsed as a result of excessive alcohol and drugs. The Stones were ruthless. "The Stones didn't fuck around. They just dumped him in a taxi. It really fucked Bobby up for a long time."

Also in 1973, the Stones' regular photographer Michael Cooper died of a drugs overdose. He took the 3D photograph for the cover of *Their Satanic Majesties' Request* and was present during the Redlands drugs bust.

Stones producer Jimmy Miller also broke down on them and later died a premature death.

"THERE ISN'T ONE PRODUCER WHO CAN HANDLE THE WHOLE THING. YOU RUN THROUGH THEM LIKE YOU RUN THROUGH GAS IN YOUR CAR. YOU BURN THEM OUT. IT'S A RUTHLESS CIRCLE. JIMMY WENT IN A LION AND CAME OUT A LAMB. WE WORE HIM OUT COMPLETELY…JIMMY ENDED UP CARVING SWASTIKAS INTO THE WOODEN CONSOLE AT THE STUDIO. IT TOOK HIM THREE MONTHS TO CARVE A SWASTIKA…"

– KEITH

Keith Harwood was a top recording engineer who worked with the Stones on two albums. In 1977, Harwood engineered the New York mixing sessions for The Rolling Stones' *Love You Live* album. He died soon after when he left a recording session and passed out from drugs at the wheel of his car. The car crashed and Harwood was killed instantly. The Rolling Stones dedicated *Love You Live* to the memory of Harwood.

Said Tony Sanchez: "At each death people said much the same thing. That's what comes of living too close to the Stones. In the end you try and live just like them. The Stones use people up..."

Ian Stewart, the "Sixth Rolling Stone", died at age 47. Ian was the keyboard player for the original Stones line-up. Oldham decided that his conservative look didn't fit with the band's image and demoted him to road manager and background keyboards. Most musicians would have balked at this insult, but Stewart actually decided that the arrangement suited him just fine and so he played a background role in most of the Stones' work between 1964 and 1983.

While enjoying a background role with the Stones, he managed to stay aloof from the band's lifestyle. "I think he looked upon it as a load of silliness," said Mick Taylor. Stewart was clearly a popular member of the band and Keith recalls them often regretting the fact that they had let the golf-mad Scot arrange parts of their tour:

"WE'D BE PLAYING IN SOME TOWN WHERE THERE'S ALL THESE CHICKS, AND THEY WANT TO GET LAID AND WE WANT TO LAY THEM. BUT STU WOULD HAVE BOOKED US INTO SOME HOTEL ABOUT TEN MILES OUT OF TOWN. YOU'D WAKE UP IN THE MORNING AND THERE'S THE LINKS. WE'RE BORED TO DEATH LOOKING FOR SOME ACTION AND STU'S PLAYING GLENEAGLES."

– KEITH

At his funeral Keith was heard lamenting, "Who's going to tell us off now when we misbehave?"

Despite the deaths and setbacks, Keith takes a philosophical view of events:

"I've relied on accidents all my life. Everything I've ever planned has never worked out. I'm just something that accidents happen to. Some of them are good, and some of them are bad. Most of them are good, and the bad ones haven't killed me yet."

If Keith is someone that accidents happen to, then Keith Moon, the former drummer of The Who, was someone who actively went out of his way to create new accidents.

"Moon the Loon" was diagnosed with a borderline personality disorder and it showed. In everything from his playing style to his lifestyle, Keith Moon just epitomised destruction. If you ever wondered who started the trend for trashing hotel rooms, you need look no further than Mr Moon. One famous story about Keith occurred during a US tour when Keith had overslept due to some serious excess the night before. The tour bus had been waiting for ages to Keith to appear and when there was no sign of him, one of the roadies was dispatched to fetch him. A few minutes later, a bleary-eyed Keith staggered onto the coach and collapsed on the first seat.

The bus had already been on the road for 20 minutes when Keith suddenly leapt to his feet and started shouting,

"WAIT, WAIT – I'VE FORGOTTEN SOMETHING!"

The tour bus returned to the hotel and Keith, apologising profusely, got the duty manager to re-open his room. Before anyone could comprehend what was happening, Keith had ripped the TV off its stand, walked over to the balcony and hurled the TV into the swimming pool below.

"Thanks very much," said Keith and casually left the room. Classy!

HOW TO BE WILD

If you`re going to be wild, it`s probably best if your liquid assets meet your liquid consumption. Don't put some scheming bastard in charge of your finances. Find yourself someone with a ludicrous name, a dodgy royal title and impeccable financial pedigree. Let him be the sensible one. Let him be sensible for all of you and then find another sensible person to check on his numbers and another one to check on his numbers... until you have formed a vicious circle of accountants. (There, I've just invented a new collective noun.)

For as long as there has been music, there have been groupies wanting to sleep with the stars. From Elgar to Elvis, there have been women wanting to take it from the top one more time. When the Stones first started, they were one of the first British bands to attract hordes of screaming girls. There was something very un-British about this phenomenon. Previously, English gals had worn gloves and patent leather shoes and applauded politely at the end of each song. Suddenly they were hurling their pants at the stage with phone numbers attached and screaming throughout the concert.

"WE GET PAID IN FLESH. OUR AUDIENCES ARE SLUTS AND WHORES, EACH AND EVERY ONE."
– NIKKI SIXX OF MOTLEY CRUE, 1984

Keith described the sound of a thousand hysterical teenagers at their early concerts as "a sort of hysterical wail, a weird sound that hundreds of chicks make when they're coming ... They sounded like hundreds of orgasms at once. They couldn't even hear the music, and we couldn't hear the music we were playing."

"It was living *A Hard Day's Night* climbing over the rooftops, with chief constables who didn't know their way, getaways down fire escapes, through laundry chutes, into bakery vans. It was all mad."

Nick Kent, a leading music journalist, witnessed the hysteria at first hand as a teenager: "You could see the whole audience change when The Rolling Stones came on. These young girls just became wild and violent and made this weird, bestial sound. It was an electrifying experience. I had front-row seats and this girl from the third row threatened me with a stiletto so I immediately sat in the third row."

If the Stones built a reputation as ladykillers in the UK, the same couldn't be said for their first trip to the States. Keith lamented the sad lack of sex on their first tour to America. "It was very difficult, man, for cats who had done England, scoring chicks right, left and centre, to come to a country where apparently no one believed in it... In New York or LA you can always find something, but when you're in Omaha in 1964... you might as well forget it."

One time we saw some hookers but when we got closer we realized it was

MOTLEY CRUE

– James Hetfield of Metallica, 1989

"I love all women, I will never stop, I want every girl that ever lived. I fuck everything that moves and if it doesn't move... we work something out."
— Gene Simmons of KISS, 1998

While other bands make great play about their wild sexual adventures, the Stones have always been slightly more reticent. That isn't to say they haven't had their share of the groupie pie (in a manner of speaking). In the early days, the band had a habit of sharing their girlfriends around. The somewhat inappropriately-named Marianne Faithfull slept with both Keith and Brian Jones before settling on Mick:

"... in the beginning I was always really in love with Keith much more than anyone else, as a fan. He's the epitome of the Romantic Hero and, if you're a middle class girl and you've read your Byron, that's Keith Richards... He's turned into Count Dracula but he's still an injured, tortured, damned youth... That's the thing about the Stones. That they're dirty and awful and arrogant and Keith is still like that."

What Keith really needed in his youth was a counterbalance. A nice, sensible Home Counties girl to rein in his wild side, point out the error of his ways and encourage his creative side. He didn't get one. What he got instead was Anita Pallenberg. If Anita Pallenberg were a car she'd be an Aston Martin V6 with seriously faulty brakes (OK, make that a Lexus). She was fast, beautiful, classy, sophisticated and sleek, but she was also a serious accident just waiting to happen. And with Anita, you didn't have to wait too long for the accidents to happen.

"I'M NOT GOD BUT IF I WERE GOD, THREE-QUARTERS OF YOU WOULD BE GIRLS, AND THE REST WOULD BE PIZZA AND BEER." – AXL ROSE OF GUNS N' ROSES, 1989

Pallenberg, like so many women associated with the Stones over the years, began a relationship with one Stone — in this case Brian Jones — then ended up with Keith, with a short detour through Mick. Only 19 years old when she met Brian Jones, Pallenberg was a German-Italian actress and model and in the early days of the Stones, she had a strong influence over the style of the band and their public image.

Chrissie Shrimpton: "Anita was very aware of her power but she was very compassionate. Unlike the other girls who were trying to steal my place (as Jagger's girlfriend), I never felt that way about Anita... She could have been evil, perhaps, because she was so very powerful, but what I liked about her was that she didn't use her power in an evil way. She was very weird and freaky and strong but her feelings were genuine."

Others were not quite so certain of her compassionate nature.

"I THOUGHT SHE WAS EVIL AND MANIPULATIVE AND WICKED."
– GERED MANKOWITZ

"Anita made me uncomfortable... there was something disturbing about her. She liked to mess with people. Her attitude was 'Come into my web and we'll play a little game'." — Nick Kent

However, all agreed on one thing — she was one extremely intelligent lady.

In Keith's words: "She knew everything and she could say it in five languages. She scared the pants off me."

So this was the woman that would be the main influence on Keith's life from the mid-1960s to 1980.

Of course, there was nothing straightforward about any aspect of their relationship. As mentioned earlier, Keith didn't even have to go out and find her. She was already dating Brian Jones when they first met. Keith stole Pallenberg from Jones during their Tour de France in 1968 and this humiliation was probably one of the key factors in the decline of Jones that led to his eventual death.

In contrast, the first few years of the Keith/Anita relationship were spectacularly successful... if you feel that becoming a junkie while simultaneously producing major best-selling albums is a reasonable definition of success.

Of course, all good things must come to an end. In the case of Anita, they didn't end quickly, they just slowly crumbled away, along with her looks and fame. It would be hard to find a more self-destructive person than Pallenberg. Tragedy and chaos followed her everywhere she went, most of it of her own making:

>> Even though she admitted to never being a big fan of Mick, she is still reputed to have shagged him for real on the set of *Performance*. Some of the scenes from the film were so explicit that they were destroyed by the processing lab, which said they contravened the obscenity laws.

"For a few years then we were just flying. We had everything – money, power, looks, protection, we had the lot."
–Pallenberg

"I COULD NEVER QUITE UNDERSTAND COCAINE. YOU CAN'T GET A HARD ON, YOU CAN'T SLEEP AND YOU GRIND YOUR TEETH, WHAT THE FUCK IS GOOD ABOUT THAT?"

– JON BON JOVI, 2000

>> Even while pregnant with their first child Marlon, Pallenberg continued to use drugs. As the pair became addicted to heroin they surrounded themselves with other heroin users, creating a self-perpetuating circle of addiction. While other R 'n' R icons brag about their sexual conquests, this simply wasn't the case with Keith. Heroin was destroying everything, including Keith's sex drive. At the height of their heroin addiction Anita used to humiliate Keith in public by screaming that he hadn't shagged her in months. She also used to flirt with many of the hangers-on that were always present in the Stones' entourage in order to bait Keith.

>> In 1972 Pallenberg was pregnant again. She tried to give up heroin but failed and so entered a Swiss private clinic to help her handle the addiction and her pregnancy. Dandelion Richards was born on 17 April into one seriously dysfunctional family.

Anita: "It should have been a good time but it was difficult having children and belonging in Keith's world. We were both still on heroin... I was more interested in getting my supply than I was in looking after them. People started to condemn me as a bad person, neglecting my kids, only interested in feeding my habit.

Instead of getting them dinner, I'd go out and wander around and meet some people and spend the night in the park looking for flying saucers."

>> The Stones were limited as to the number of places they could travel to record albums because of Keith's issues. In 1972 they moved to Jamaica to record *Goat's Head Soup*. While living there, Pallenberg surrounded herself with a tough gang of local boys who were clearly servicing her in many ways. Keith left her behind with the kids and went on a self-destructive binge in London. Unfortunately for Pallenberg, the local white community had simply had enough her and she was arrested and thrown into jail where she was allegedly beaten and raped.

>> In 1976 Keith and Anita's third child, a boy called Tara, choked to death in his cot. Nick Kent speculated that Keith loved Anita but had reached a point where he realised, 'Baby, I can't carry you anymore, you've gone crazy'.

>> On 20 July 1979, a 17-year-old boy called Scott Cantrell blew his head off with one of Keith's handguns at Pallenberg's home in Salem, New York. Keith, who was in Paris at the time, told Anita that this was the last straw. Eventually, Anita was cleared of any involvement in Cantrell's death and was given a conditional discharge. However, the boy's father told the press: "I think they were lovers and she had supplied him with drugs. A 37-year-old woman should have known better than to associate with a 17-year-old boy in her bedroom. I feel she is fully responsible for the death of my son, no matter how they wrap it."

The year after splitting with Anita and being bust in Toronto, Keith decided to give up hard drugs. Soon after this he took up with a new girlfriend, Lilly Wenglass Green. Showing a sad lack of originality in his taste for women, Lilly was like many before: blonde, Swedish and a model. According to friends she was also extremely sexual and probably played a significant role in getting Keith back into shape following years of neglect and abuse.

"THE ABILITY FOR A WOMAN TO ORALLY SATISFY SOMEBODY IN A ROCK BAND, THAT'S IMPORTANT TO A ROCK 'N' ROLL MUSICIAN."
– CHAD KROEGER OF NICKELBACK, 2006

While there is no doubt that the Stones have bedded many exotic women over the years, there has also been a lot of speculation about the relationship between Mick and Keith. John Lennon and Paul McCartney were convinced there was something more than friendship between the two. The pair has often been described, by themselves as well as others, as being like a married couple.

Said Keith: "It's a true friendship when you can bash somebody over the head and not be told 'You're not my friend anymore'. You put up with each other's bitching... He's my wife. And he'll say the same thing about me." This has often made life difficult, especially when their real partners have tried to assert their influence. Keith was not a big fan of either of Mick's first two wives — Bianca Jagger and Jerry

Hall. Throughout the 1980s, the pair of them drifted apart as Jerry Hall became the dominant person in Mick's life.

At around the same time Keith met the American model, Patti Hansen, who was to play a major part in his life. When they first met at Studio 54, she swears she didn't

"Drugs and sex go hand in hand when you're a rock and roll musician. Whereas if I were a violinist, it might be a little different."

"I'M A FAMILY ORIENTED GUY; I'VE PERSONALLY STARTED FOUR OR FIVE THIS YEAR."
– DAVID LEE ROTH OF VAN HALEN, 1982

exactly know who he was. She was 23 and he was 36. "I knew who the Rolling Stones were," she says, "but I didn't listen to that music. I loved the Supremes, Smokey Robinson — soul." However, she quickly became smitten. "I just loved this man," she says. "I loved the way he looked, his eyes, his strength — everything about him."

Even Patti's brother was impressed by his wild sister's new boyfriend: "I knew she had made the right choice. He's so different from what you expect. I was amazed at what a well-mannered, intelligent, poetic man he is. They are a perfect match — both are blunt, bold, no-bullshit people."

On 18 December 1983, Keith and Patti got married. Keith chose the date to coincide with his birthday so that he wouldn't forget the anniversary. As you would expect of Keith, the honeymoon wasn't quite the romantic getaway that Patti might have had in mind. They were picked up at the airport in Jamaica by some of Keith's 'rude boy' friends who, smoking joints on the way, managed to run over a goat. They had to flee the scene as gun-toting villagers chased them for compensation. As they arrived at the safety of Keith's mansion they heard screaming coming from the swimming pool. Keith had to dash out and save Freddy Sessler, who was drowning in the swimming pool.

Despite these early hiccups in the marriage, Keith and Patti have remained married and content ever since and have two daughters, Theodora and Alexandra.

We all know that anyone can be saved by the love of a good woman. But remember, you have already sold your soul to the devil. How can one woman, working alone, possibly hope to save your soul? Clearly, you will be needing the love of many good women to save you from the fires of eternal damnation. Think of it as a religious duty to secure the love of as many good women as possible, in as many ways as possible (you need to cover all the bases). I'm certain the Catholic Church would approve.

Share and Share Alike. The Stones built their foundations on a Three Musketeers philosophy. "All for One and One for All" could have been their mission statement. There's no point in being selfish about your women. If you're onto a good thing, share the goodness around! This can only help build team spirit within the band. If you take a look at *groupiedirt.com* you will see that many bands are happy to help out a friend in need. Why, you and a band member could even find yourselves the considerate provider of a "spit roast" to one of your adoring fans. No explanations offered or required.

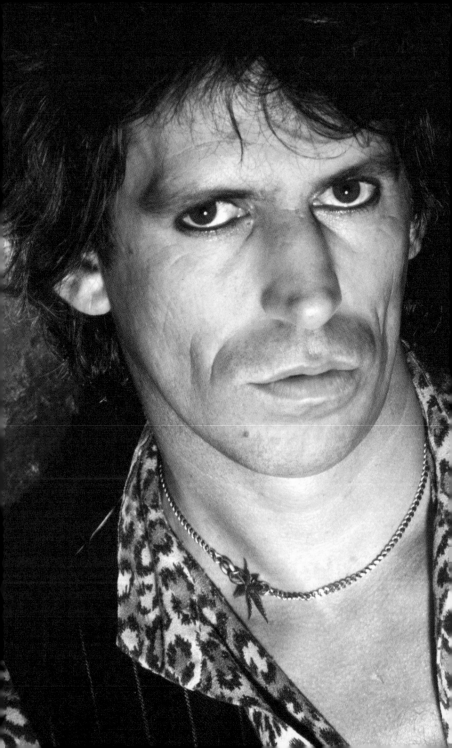

In the 1960s, good drugs and free lovin' were seen as the path to an enlightened world full of happy, smiley people wearing paisley kaftans and Jesus sandals with a reckless compulsion to hug you. The only thing standing between us and that sick, cruel world was the thin blue line of the law. Frankly speaking, people just aren't grateful enough for the good work of the police.

Leading the drugs section of the Age of Aquarius was Keith and the boys (Momas and Papas were leading the flowery kaftan section and they didn't fare any better in the long run. Had there been a decent law for Crimes Against Clothing, many of the '60s bands would have received life sentences).

"I've never had a problem with drugs. I've had problems with the POLICE."

— Keith

The Rolling Stones Drugs Tour T-Shirt

1967 The Redlands Bust!

1968 Brian Jones for speed, coke and hashish

1969 Mick Jagger and Marianne Faithfull
      for hashish

1972 Keith in France – coke, hashish, heroin

1972 Anita Pallenberg in Jamaica
      for marijuana

1973 Keith for cannabis, heroin, mandrax
      and ... (drum roll) ... unregistered guns
      (ker-ching!)

1975 Keith and Ronnie for cocaine in Texas

1976 Keith for cocaine and LSD

1977 The Toronto Bust! Keith and Anita in
      Canada for heroin and hashish

1980 Ronnie in St Maarten for cocaine

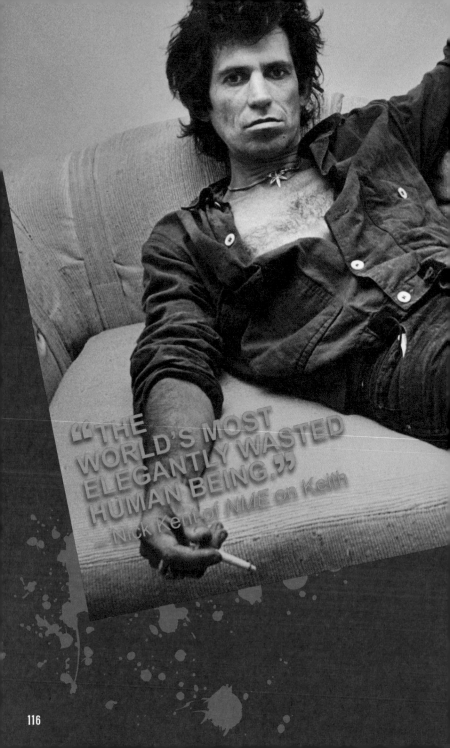

"THE WORLD'S MOST ELEGANTLY WASTED HUMAN BEING."
— Nick Kent of *NME* on Keith

In his autobiography **Life**, Keith reflects on his life as a heroin addict.

"The life of being a junkie is not recommended to anybody. I was on the top end, and that was pretty low. It's certainly not the road to musical genius or anything else. It was a balancing act. I've got loads of things to do, this song's interesting, and I want to make copies of all this stuff, and I'd be doing it for five days, perfectly balanced in this equilibrium of cocaine and heroin."

Richards explained to the journalist Nick Kent in an interview that drugs are used by many musicians as a practical way of staying awake and alert when you are on the road. "You reach a point very early on when you're sitting around in the dressing room with some other acts in the show and you say 'I've gotta drive 500 miles and do two shows tomorrow and can't make it'. And so you look around at the other guys and say 'How the hell have you been making it for all these years?' And they say, 'Well baby take one of these'."

"It's a matter of making the next gig. Like the bomber pilots — if you've got to bomb Dresden tomorrow, you get, like, four or five bennies to make the trip and keep yourself together. 'Do you want me to crash this sucker, or do you want me to stay awake?' 'Here Squadron Leader, open up your mouth and I'll pop a couple of these blighters in.' I'm sure it was really good speed those fuckers got as well. Government issue. That's how it starts out, and it's usually speed. And once you've got past that, the next question is an escalation."

Sadly for Keith, the law didn't quite understand the practical nature of his drug habit and took to busting him on regular occasions. Keith was first busted in 1967 when police raided his house at Redlands in West Wittering on the English south coast and found amphetamines in the coat pocket of Jagger's girlfriend, Marianne Faithfull. Keith and Mick were convicted and sentenced to a year in prison. There was a public outcry over the harshness of the sentence, including a famous editorial from William Rees-Mogg in The Times entitled *Who Breaks a Butterfly on a Wheel?*

"If we are going to make any case a symbol of the conflict between the sound traditional values of Britain and the new hedonism, then we must be sure that the sound traditional values include those of tolerance and equity. It should be the particular quality of British justice to ensure that Mr Jagger is treated exactly the same as anyone else, no better and no worse. There must remain a suspicion in this case that Mr Jagger received a more severe sentence than would have been thought proper for any purely anonymous young man."

The Court's decision was overturned and a hugely relieved Keith and Mick were released. However, the police weren't prepared to be quite so forgiving. Throughout the '60s and '70s, Keith was harassed constantly by the police wherever he went. In the UK it simply got ridiculous: "It was literally a case of the police saying, "Well old Sergeant Jim and his wife need a new three-piece suite. We'll go down to Keith Richard's place... cause you know... there's going to be drugs there. Is there going to be something illegal there? Of course there is."

"THE ENGLISH POLICE ARE POLITELY SARKY. LIKE 'ELLO KEITHY MY BOY, OLD LAD, OLD CHUM, YOU KNOW THE RULES OF THE GAME.' VERY BUDDY-BUDDY BUT WE'RE STILL GOING TO DO YOU."

— KEITH

> **We've all got our self-destructive bad habits, the trick is to find four or five you personally like the best and just do those all the time.**
> — David Lee Roth of Van Halen, 1980

In 1971, just before he joined the Stones at Nellcote in the south of France, Keith decided he needed to visit Anita, who was undergoing a traumatic detox programme in Harrow. To prepare for the journey, Keith drank a few margaritas and snorted a line of coke before jumping into his car for the journey to Harrow. Now most people who are a little over the legal driving limit might proceed quietly, slowly and discreetly to avoid drawing attention to themselves. Clearly deciding that attack was the best form of defence, Keith jumped into his psychedelic pink Bentley and took off like a bat out of hell with the external speakers on his car blaring out the Stones' latest album, *Sticky Fingers*.

Amazingly, Keith got to within a few miles of his destination without incident, when his luck ran out. Swerving to avoid an oncoming truck, Keith slammed into a traffic island and destroyed the Bentley. Keith and his mate Michael Cooper decided that it was probably best if they weren't around when the police arrived. Dashing off down a side road, they eventually found a small house with a front garden where they decided they should bury their stash of drugs.

Just as they were shoving the last piece of earth onto the stash, the house door opened and a surprised Stones session musician called Nicky Hopkins stepped out of the

"There was a time
I thought I couldn't enjoy
rock 'n' roll unless I had
heroin in me."

— Joe Perry of Aerosmith, 1989

house to invite them in for a drink! Another fine example of the Devil's luck enjoyed by Mr Richards.

In 1972, Keith and the boys were raided by the police at Nellcote, as was his British residence the following year. A French court gave him a one-year suspended sentence, a $1,000 fine and banned him from entering France for two years.

On the 1975 tour, the band were worried that Keith wouldn't be allowed a visa for their US tour. Mick used his connections with the UK Embassy to get a visa clearance. They were given the all-clear provided Keith could return a clear blood sample. Keith returned to his Swiss clinic for a blood transfusion and the visa was granted. On arriving in the US, they were approached in their suite by two large men who identified themselves as FBI. They explained that they knew of his drug problems and that the car sponsor for their tour was worried about negative publicity, should he be caught with drugs. Therefore, they explained that they would ensure he had an ample supply of heroin for the duration of the tour.

What a sound and practical solution to the problem! If only all other countries could have been so practical and sensible.

"I'VE NEVER TURNED BLUE IN SOMEONE ELSE'S BATHROOM. I CONSIDER THAT THE HEIGHT OF BAD MANNERS."

– KEITH

Said Nick Kent: "In the '70s it was really about Keith and the danger around Keith. He lived, and continues to live, an incredibly dangerous life and he doesn't give a fuck. He lives his life like it's a movie. Keith Richards was the Godfather. Everyone wanted to be like Keith Richards. He was the big Lord Byron figure. He was mad, bad and dangerous to know..."

On their European tour in 1976 Keith started to look terrible, no longer the handsome young guy that had excited so many women early in his career. During one concert in Germany he actually fell asleep on stage while playing *Fool to Cry*. The American leg of the tour wasn't much better with the Stones being constantly harassed by the police as they passed from state to state (literally and metaphorically!).

Keith: "You're being harassed from every quarter and it becomes a war. Wherever you went you were subject to the same controls, the same body searches... and eventually when you got cocky enough you'd still walk out carrying (drugs) because they're so bad at their job, and you'd get off on that. But it's a minor victory because eventually, of course, they're going to get you..."

"Of course what I had has a certain appeal to people — everybody would have liked to have lived like that once in a while... to be able to do that 'Fuck you!' thing. But the romantic myth that applied was not very romantic to me. I had to go through it."

"Cocaine is like really evil coffee."
— Courtney Love

Keith had many run-ins with the law over the years but the closest he came to being put away for drugs offences was in Toronto. In February 1977, the Stones flew into Toronto. Keith was carrying a small quantity of hashish but the Canadian police had obviously been tipped off about something bigger. It turned out Keith had arranged for some drugs to be sent to him by mail and it's possible these had been intercepted, then sent on again in order to trap him. Whatever, Keith was woken by 15 members of the Canadian Mounted Police who quickly found Keith's stash of drugs.

In October 1978, Keith went on trial in Toronto for possession of 22g of heroin. Huge crowds gathered outside chanting "Free Keith". Keith's lawyer, Austin Cooper, based his defence on testimony from a stream of witnesses who declared that Keith had kicked his drug habit in the last year. "I ask Your Honour to understand him as a tortured creative person... He turned to heroin to prop up a sagging existence. I ask you to understand the whole man." He also promised that Keith would donate US$1 million to a rehabilitation clinic.

Lemmy Kilmister of Motorhead made an important and interesting observation about uniforms in a 2004 interview with Waste Music:

"The bad guys always had the best uniforms. Napoleon, the Confederates, the Nazis. They all had killer uniforms. I mean, the SS uniform is fucking brilliant! They were the rock stars of the time. What you gonna do? They just look good."

During the trial, a friend of Keith's was quoted as saying: "The problem with Keith is he thinks rock 'n' roll is real life. He's the most naïve person I know."

"WE BELIEVED THAT ANYTHING THAT WAS WORTH DOING WAS WORTH OVERDOING."
– STEVEN TYLER OF AEROSMITH, 1990

The judge's verdict was one year's probation, no fine, no jail; a pledge to maintain his good behaviour; report to a probation officer on specified dates; to continue his treatment; and to give a concert for the Canadian Institute for the Blind (CNIB) within six months.

While Keith's lenient sentence was probably due to good work from his lawyer, Keith also credited an intervention from his "Blind Angel":

"This little chick from Toronto was totally blind, but there was nothing that would stop this girl from turning up at gigs. So I'd fix her up, give the girl a ride, 'cause I just had visions of her being run over. God knows what could happen to a blind chick on the road. This chick went to the judge's house in Toronto, personally, and she told him this simple story. And from there he figured out a way to get Canada and himself and myself out of the whole mess."

Richards performed two CNIB benefit concerts at Oshawa Civic Auditorium on 22 April 1979. Both shows featured The Rolling Stones and Ronnie Wood & Keith's solo project **The New Barbarians**. They raised US$50,000 for the Institute.

"I never thought I was
wasted, but I probably was."
— Keith

The Toronto bust was actually the wake-up call that Keith needed and he decided that he needed to clean himself up. "I just knew I had to finish with dope. It was a traumatic event that reshaped the rest of my life... It was either put the lid on it or you're going to live in the big house for quite a while."

"I've been an amateur chemist, a 'drugologist'. I always went by this old 1903 medical dictionary which was produced before drugs were considered bad for you. If you were constipated you were told to go to the chemists and get a little tincture of cocaine. If you had diarrhea, then it was a gram of heroin. I've abused drugs but I didn't go into them without boning up on them first."

"Never take ecstasy, beer, Bacardi, weed, Pepto Bismol, Vivarin, Tums, Tagamet, HB, Xanax and Valium in the same day. It makes it really difficult to sleep at night."

— Eminem

"I WAS THE PISS ARTIST, BARRY WAS THE POTHEAD AND ROBIN WAS THE PILLHEAD."

– MICHAEL GIBB OF THE BEE GEES

After meeting Patti Hansen in 1979, Keith enjoyed a period of relative stability. He may given up hard drugs but his lifestyle didn't change that much. "I'd been up for nine days. I was working on something in the studio and I put a tape in the machine to hear the latest blast I'd gotten. I turned around and fell asleep for a millisecond and I collapsed into the corner of a JBL speaker. You know what noses are like. Great nap, waking to this red shower. I think I gave it a slight curve to the left. It was just that life was so interesting for nine days that I couldn't give it up. Not even for a minute."

"It's an addiction... and addiction is something I should know something about."
– Keith

Spend a lot of time in the bathroom. Keith spent most of the 1970s in bathrooms, with just an occasional break to go touring. Most of the time the Stones were at Nellcote they were hanging around waiting for Mick and Anita Pallenberg to come out of the bathroom and play.

Interestingly, bathrooms seem to play a major role in the lives of many Wild Men. In an interview with *Rolling Stone* magazine Russell Brand described how "Throughout my life I've found myself in lavatories. As a kid I would play in them and break stuff, and then there was that period of bulimia and puking; and then there's masturbation; and then there's drug addiction and bathrooms in train stations, airplanes, cafes and bars; and then, once I came off drugs, there was loads of sex in bathrooms, because when you're sleeping with five or six women a day, that's where a lot of it happens. And then, before gigs, I'd go to the bathroom just to empty myself out… Of course I was, generally speaking, a little more of a lackadaisical, frivolous person back then, whereas now I'm just pretty pompous."

HOW TO BE HIGH

It would be wildly irresponsible of anyone to suggest that mind altering substances could in any way enhance your musical creativity...

Absolutely not. I prefer to let the rock legends speak for themselves. Huge names in the industry such as The Osmonds and Olivia Newton-John have "Just said NO to Drugs", while others taking a somewhat alternative view of the situation include Keith, the Beatles, Slash, Iggy Pop, Amy Winehouse, Eminem, Louis Armstrong, Jimi Hendrix, The Grateful Dead, Fleetwood Mac, David Bowie...

You be the judge.

Rock 'n' roll didn't just change the face of music in the 20th century, it played a major part in reshaping society and established the youth market as a separate subculture.

Teenagers no longer just become mini-me's of their parents when they grew up — they had their own fashions, language and musical tastes. It was no coincidence that the expression **Rock 'n' Roll** came from black American slang for sex in the 1930s. Basically, rock 'n' roll ripped the pants off 1950s society and gave it a good seeing to. According to Keith, this was more than appropriate:

"MUSIC HAS ALWAYS SEEMED STREETS AHEAD OF ANY OTHER ART FORM OR ANY OTHER FORM OF SOCIAL EXPRESSION. AFTER AIR, FOOD, WATER AND FUCKING, I THINK MAYBE MUSIC IS THE NEXT HUMAN NECESSITY. PEOPLE THINK MUSIC IS A LUXURY. IN ACTUAL FACT, MUSIC IS A NECESSITY, BECAUSE IT'S THE ONE THING THAT WILL MAYBE BRING YOU UP AND GIVE YOU JUST THAT LITTLE BIT EXTRA TO KEEP ON GOING."

> ## "JAZZ—ISN'T THAT JUST A SERIES OF MISTAKES DISGUISED AS MUSICAL COMPOSITION?"
>
> – DAVID ST. HUBBINS OF SPINAL TAP, 1992

Although the Stones' early inspiration came from US Blues players such as **Muddy Waters** and **Robert Johnson**, it took a long time for the conservative Americans to come round to enjoying the music of the Stones. On their first trip to the States, Richards enthused: "Nobody realises how America blew our minds. I can't even describe what America meant to us. How can you measure it? We were all enthralled and turned on with the idea of being in America, fairyland... Once I got to the Astor Hotel it became a blur that day because we just went berserk..."

However, their short tour was not all they had hoped it would be. They were insulted on TV by Dean Martin, who on the completion of their set said, "The Rolling Stones... aren't they great?", and then rolled his eyes theatrically.

Many of their concerts were poorly attended, especially in the Midwest. They were also harassed by the police on a regular basis. Backstage at one concert, a cop pulled a gun on Richards after he refused to pour his Coke down the toilet. The irony was that (for a change) Keith was only drinking Coke and it was the other band members who were drinking whisky and Coke.

> ## Music is part of us, and it either ennobles or degrades our behavior.
> ### — M.S. Bothus,
> ### Sixth century musician

The Stones were not only unusual in that they were a bunch of white guys playing their own version of rhythm and blues from the American south, they also managed to put their own unique spin on it.

Bill Wyman: "Every rock 'n' roll band follows the drummer. If the drummer slows down, the band slows down with him or speeds up when he does. That's just the way it works — except for our band. Our band doesn't follow the drummer; our drummer follows the rhythm guitarist, who is Keith Richards. It's probably a matter of personality. Keith is a very confident and stubborn player. Immediately you've got something like a hundredth-of-a-second delay between the guitar and Charlie's lovely drumming, and that will change the sound completely... when you actually hear that it seems to just pulse. You know it's right because we're all making stops and starts and it's in time — but it isn't as well. The net result is that loose type of pulse that goes down between Keith, Charlie and me."

Nik Kohn: "They lay down something very violent in the lines of rhythm and blues... They were mean and nasty, full blooded, very testy, and they beat out the toughest crudest, most offensive noise an English band had ever made... Naughty but nice, they were liked by the Aldermaston marchers and hitchhikers, beards and freaks and preanderthal Mods everywhere. Simply, they were turning in to the voice of hooliganism... Keith Richards wore T-shirts; he was shut in, shuffling, the classic school dropout. Simply he spelled Borstal."

Even Chuck Berry was forced to admit that the Stones guitarist had something special to offer: " His playing was raw and raunchy with unrelenting energy. My playing captured the spirit of teenage rebellion in the 1950s and Keith, to his credit, updated it with a 1960s sound. The music started sounding hotter, more dangerous. He'd push out the same feeling I'd given it, without ever losing that adolescent soul."

"I MEAN, THIS IS SERIOUS. IT'S MY MUSIC AFFECTING THE LIVES OF PEOPLE YOU DON'T EVEN KNOW, WHICH IS DEFINITELY A SCARY THING TO HAVE THAT MUCH POWER."
– SLASH OF GUNS 'N' ROSES

"In a sense, music is not made by the fully rational, fully conscious human being; part of a musician's training is to 'get out of the way' and let the music flow through. The perfect artist is one whose individual human characteristics are as good as turned off — the nearer to 'not there' they are, the more the music can take command. Alcohol and drugs are a shortcut to removing many of the properties of consciousness." — **Dick Heckstall-Smith** of John Mayall Band

While many saw the Stones' music in the 1960s as the beginning of a Renaissance in music, not everybody felt the same way:

Keith: "I've never been hated by so many people I've met as in Nebraska in the mid-'60s. You could just tell they wanted to beat the shit out of you."

By the time the 1970s rolled around, the Stones were established as one of the leading bands in the world, with massive audiences wherever they played. However, their offstage antics led them very close to falling into the abyss. Although Keith was addicted to heroin, he prided himself on always being able to perform, no matter what state he was in. Some nights were better than others. Said Keith: "I did get to a point where the music was secondary. I was devoting most of my time to scoring and taking dope. I was completely out of it and Mick had to cover for me. He took over completely. I managed to make gigs and write some songs but Mick took care of everything through most of the '70s. The cat worked his butt off. He covered my ass. I feel I owe Mick. I've always admired him very much for that."

In 1972, Anita Pallenberg commented on Keith & Mick during one of their "down" times. "They've always got this kind of battle going on. They had to have friction. They couldn't just sit there because they're such opposites. Mick believes in going into the studio with a sheet of paper and all the notes written. And Keith, he goes into the studio and it's just childhood play."

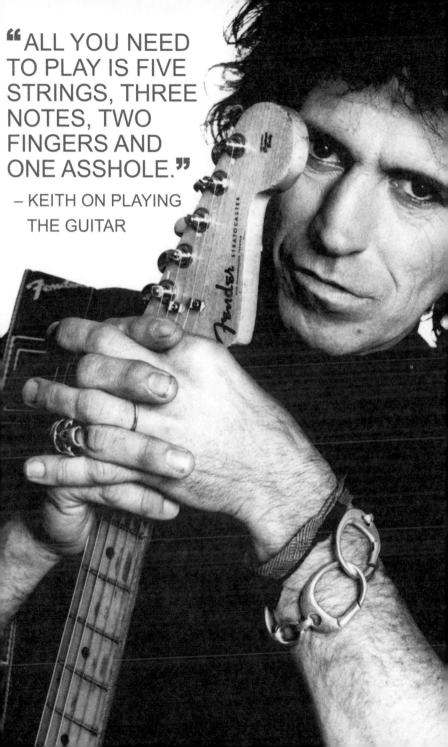

"ALL YOU NEED TO PLAY IS FIVE STRINGS, THREE NOTES, TWO FINGERS AND ONE ASSHOLE."

– KEITH ON PLAYING THE GUITAR

Music has charms to soothe the savage breast, or so it's said. However, this may not always be the case. The songwriter for the classic song Pack All Your Troubles in Your Old Kit Bag and Smile, Smile, Smile actually committed suicide in the midst of World War II.

While it's easy to focus on Keith's wild side, it should never be forgotten that he is also one of the greatest rock guitarists of his generation. He has always been keen to experiment with his playing skills and introduced open tunings into his repertoire in the late '60s. Open tuning describes the tuning of a guitar so that a chord is achieved without fretting, or pressing any of the strings. This style of tuning is especially popular for slide and blues guitarists.

Keith also plays most Stones' songs with only five strings on his guitar, preferring a five-string variant of open G-tuning using GDGBD and losing the low sixth string. In an interview with *Guitar World* magazine, he joked that while he played a wide range of guitars, "give me five minutes and I'll make 'em all sound the same".

The advent of punk was an interesting event for the Stones. From being the class rebels, the Stones suddenly found themselves being criticised by the punk bands as being soft and mainstream. "Groups like the Stones are revolting," said Johnny Rotten of the Sex Pistols. Johnny's buddy Sid Vicious was even more poetic: "I wouldn't piss on Keith Richards if he was on fire."

In 1980, when Keith was in his recovery period, not everyone was happy. Now that he was back in control he wanted to take control of the Stones again.

Keith talking about Mick: "OK now I'm ready to shoulder some of the burden again. God bless you for taking it all on your shoulders when I was out there playing the freaked-out artist and getting busted — he (Mick) supported me every fucking inch of the way. I ain't knocking the cat at all. But when I came back, I didn't want to believe that Mick was enjoying the burden. He could now control the whole thing; it became a power trip. I heard that shit from the john like 'I wish he was a junkie again.'"

In 1981, the Stones hit the road again. Their US tour from September to December of that year grossed US$50 million and was watched by three million people. However, band members Ronnie Wood and Bobby Keys were suffering from serious drug problems. For someone who had only recently expelled his own demons, Keith could be particularly tough on the two errant band members.

"There's one boy (Ronnie) who hasn't got much longer the way he's going," he told one journalist at the time.

However, the early 1980s were a golden time for the Stones. The cleaned-up Keith was playing better than ever and the band received excellent reviews wherever they played.

Robert Palmer: "The Stones of the '80s seem to have a handle on who they are, and a clear understanding of who they aren't. They aren't kids, or rebel anarchists or demons anymore. But they're still supremely self-confident, even a little arrogant; they're still a rock 'n' roll band."

The success of the *Tattoo You* tour was a turning point. It re-established the Stones as the world's greatest rock 'n' roll band. The media were extravagant in their praise and especially of Jagger who was acclaimed as "the greatest businessman in rock and roll history". This acclaim came at the same time as they decided to renegotiate their distribution contract for Rolling Stone records.

Jagger took full advantage of their position to negotiate an excellent deal for the Stones but also negotiated two solo albums for himself. This was the beginning of a rift between Keith and Mick that was to last for the next five years.

Said Keith: "He was spending more time doing his solo stuff instead of doing *Dirty Work*, which really pissed me off. He shouldn't have been making the album if he wasn't into it. I very nearly stiffed him at the time. But there's no joy in punching a wimp. I like him and I say these things, and they come out and they sound kind of cruel, but I've known Mick since I was four years old and despite myself I do love the guy."

Bill Wyman also shoved the knife in: "I've lost touch with whoever Mick is now. I'm sure he has as well. Seven or eight years ago I could talk to Mick about books, films and intelligent things but now I just talk to him in asides... He's not my boss. We are a band and Keith Richards runs the Rolling Stones, really. Mick is a brilliant man but in the final count he has just his share of five votes and no more."

Ronnie Woods: "A few times Keith and I felt like killing people but we picked up our guitars and wrote songs instead... We've all been spared long jail sentences by being able to play our music."

In 1986, Keith got the chance to play with one of his heroes, Chuck Berry, in a documentary about the rock 'n' roll legend. Tensions were high between the two as Chuck ran through his full repertoire of weird and whacky moods. At one point, things almost spilled over when Chuck pulled up Keith over his playing on a couple of songs. "Most of the band... are going 'Keith in this situation is going to pull out the blade and just slit the motherfucker's throat'. I'm biting bullets because I'm trying to show the band that, in order to get this gig together, I am going to take some shit that I wouldn't take from anybody. I'm not going to let Chuck get to me that much. Whereas anybody else, it would have been toilet time. Nobody can touch me in that way. In the film you can see I'm chewing. I'm on the edge. At any moment I could have turned around and downed the motherfucker... He's the only guy who's hit me and I haven't done anything about it. Far worse things have happened to me in my life than Chuck Berry trying to fuck with me."

Said Steve Jordan on the incident: "It didn't really matter what Chuck put him through because Keith was going to repay that debt no matter how long it took. It was something that plagued Keith. He had to document the real thing before Chuck died, and he did. Maybe I'm reading too much into it but having played with Keith before and after, I think he's more himself now, more comfortable, like he feels entitled to make his own mark."

In 1987, the band came as close as it ever had to breaking up. It was the year that Keith signed a deal with Richard Branson's Virgin Records for two solo albums. The first of these, with Keith's new band — **The X-Pensive Winos** — was the album *Talk Is Cheap*.

In January 1989, Keith decided that it was time to confront Mick over their differences. He flew to Barbados and met Mick where they then started an epic row which eventually dissolved into good natured banter and then to a resolution. The end result was a new album — *Steel Wheels* — which they recorded at Air Studios in Montserrat.

Ronnie: "When we got back together for *Steel Wheels*, the atmosphere was kind of kid gloves but there was nevertheless a happy feeling. You could see everybody breathing a sigh of relief that Mick and Keith were getting on again. Thank God!"

Keith described the mixing process for *Steel Wheels* as "Putting the fairy dust on the bastard... This music, it's certainly not Beethoven or Mozart. It's got nothing to do with intricacy. It's got to do with a bunch of guys making accidents together, spontaneity and an immediate form of communication."

The Stones went on tour to promote the *Steel Wheels* album. Before the tour started Keith had to go for a physical. "The bugger stuck electrodes all over my body, hooked up more monitors to me than the Stones use on stage, and told me I was 'normal'! I mean, can you imagine anyone telling Keith Richards he was normal!"

The tour was a success and the Stones were clearly enjoying being together again. Keith said, "You can't compete with this. I can't explain the chemistry of it. Now we're back playing, getting paid a hell of a lot of money to play our songs. To be a grouch in this position, you'd really have to be an asshole."

Keith also confessed to taking life easier on the road than he used to: **"THE IDEA OF PARTYING FOR NINE DAYS IN ORDER TO KEEP THE IMAGE OF KEITH RICHARDS UP IS STUPID. THAT WAS KEITH RICHARDS THEN. NOW I'LL STAY UP FOR JUST TWO OR THREE DAYS."**

In 1991, the Stones again faced the prospect of break-up when Bill Wyman threatened to leave the band on the back of an embarrassing break-up with his child-bride Mandy Smith. As Charlie Watts explained at the time, "Bill can't leave the Stones. It's like joining the army. You can't get out."

However, despite the best efforts from the band, Bill delisted himself from the Stones... and then there were four.

In an interview with Nick Coleman in 1990, Keith reflected on what keeps him going: "The funny thing about those riffs, those songs, is that if I'm playing them, it's because I still get the same kick out of it, y'know? ... There're riffs like *Tumbling Dice* where you go (and he kisses his hands and blows on them) Jesus *Christ* it's a sweet riff. This is the feeling I been looking for forever, *Jesus Christ is this me*!? HEY, THAT'S ME BABY AND I SOUND LIKE THIS!" And he rolls back from the edge of his seat, hands in the air, wheezing like a boiler."

"THE STONES ARE A JAZZ BAND MASQUERADING AS A ROCK 'N' ROLL BAND. WE DON'T GO INTO THE STUDIO OR WRITE SONGS IN A WAY THAT IS PRE-PLANNED OR CUT AND DRIED. IF I HAVE A SONG I'LL SAY 'HERE'S THE SKELETON, LET'S PUT THE SKIN ON IT, DRESS IT UP AND SEE WHERE THE BAND WILL TAKE IT'."

– KEITH IN 2003

HOW TO BE WILD

You can become famous with no real musical talent – thank you Sid Vicious and Mark Wahlberg – but to be recognised as a rock legend you really have to get your groove on and nurture it year after year. However, it's also impossible to do it alone. The Stones are a bit like one of those freaky, great teams like Busby's Babes, Brazil's 1970 World Cup team, the 1927 New York Yankees, the 1995 Chicago Bulls, Torvill and Dean… A collection of disparate personalities that came together and made magic. So get out there and look around for the best talent in your neighbourhood. Nevermind that the best are probably geeks and weirdos, they are your path to stardom, hot chicks, drunken excess,

Looking back on the 1960s and remembering all the drama around the Rolling Stones — the drug busts, the prison sentences, the garish tabloid headlines — it's easy to forget just how shocked people were by the Stones' behaviour. What the fogeys of the time failed to realise was that these guys weren't trying to change the world, they just wanted to have a good time. As Mick said in an interview at the time, **"FIGHT THE ESTABLISHMENT? WE JUST WANTED TO BE FREE!"**

Put yourself in the Stones' position: you're young, good looking (OK, three out of five are anyway), you're making great music, you have money, you have millions of screaming, adoring fans and you are in the middle of one of the most free-wheeling periods in mankind's history. Hell, you would be an idiot if you didn't go crazy.

The Stones were simply the right guys in the right place at the right time. Their music and their message struck a chord and they became the mouthpiece for a whole generation. A flyer from Oakland, California in the late '60s read:

"The Bastards hear us playing you on our little transistor radios and know that they will not escape the blood and fire of the Anarchist revolution. We will play your music, dear Rolling Stones, in rock and roll marching bands as we tear down the jails and free the prisoners and arm the poor. Tattoo *Burn Baby Burn* on the asses of the wardens and generals."

Well good for you, young man!

Of course what has happened is that every rock 'n' roller since the '60s has felt duty-bound to follow Keith's trail of destruction. He has become the Pied Piper of Mayhem. It's got to the stage where if you don't have some sort of serious vice then nobody is going to take you seriously. You become a bit of a Justin Bieber.

So the last 50 years have seen a stream of wild men (and women) behaving badly for a good cause — their personal branding and street cred. Since this book is dealing with the wild, the crazy and the woolly of music, it would be a travesty if we weren't to focus at least one full chapter on some of the more excessive behaviour that has kept us entertained, kept the tabloid presses running and kept Betty Ford in business. In fact there is one entire industry that owes Keith a debt of gratitude. Drying-out celebrities has become big business these days and has spawned a wave of luxury treatment centres. The membership list of these places reads like a short-list for the Oscars and Emmies.

In no particular order...

Promises Treatment Center, California:
Britney Spears, Robert Downy Jr., Diana Ross and Ben Affleck

The Betty Ford Clinic, California:
Keith Urban, Ozzy Osbourne and Chevy Chase

Cirque Lodge, Utah:
Mary-Kate Olsen, Lindsay Lohan, Eva Mendes and Kirsten Dunst

Passages Rehab Facility, California:
David Hasselhoff, Andy Dick, Polly Shore and Stephen Baldwin

Caron Foundation, Pennsylvania:
Miss USA Tara Conner, Stephen Tyler of Aerosmith and American Idol and Liza Minnelli

So in honour of the industry's excesses, let's take a look at some of the more bizarre and entertaining behaviour lavished on us by some of the music industry's greatest talents.

Johnny Cash ....

Thanks to the excellent James Mangold film, *Walk the Line*, we have a pretty good idea of what the Man in Black got up to, or indeed what got into the man. Cash was a troubled guy who cultivated a rebel image which he enhanced with a series of prison concerts, culminating in the excellent *At Folsom Prison* album released in 1968.

Cash saw the inside of a jail cell on many occasions because of his drug problems but was never actually imprisoned. In 1965, he was arrested for smuggling drugs inside his guitar case but only received a suspended sentence. Somewhat bizarrely he was arrested the following year in Starkville, Mississippi, for trespassing onto a private property late at night to pick flowers. OK, so not all arrests are cool... which brings us onto George Michael...

I lied about George Michael. We have much bigger and more interesting fish to fry here my friends. Take for instance...

Jerry Lee Lewis ....

It's hard to know where to start with Jerry Lee Lewis. If there is ever a Hall of Fame for Borderline Insane Musical Psychopaths (the BIMP Awards) then King Jerry will be leading them all in. A *Rolling Stone* article in 2006 claimed that Lewis was "the only guy in all of music who makes Keith Richards look about as dangerous as Jessica Simpson..." Well, it's nice for Keith that he's seen to be the benchmark for bad behaviour.

So what exactly did Jerry "the Killer" Lewis get up to that was just so damned upsetting? Well for starters he liked his drugs. In Harry Shapiro's *Waiting for the Man* it's claimed that Jerry's habit began as a result of playing in a truck-stop bar where truckers would tip him with speed (used to keep them awake). This no doubt resulted in *A Whole Lotta Shakin' Goin' On* which made him famous and wealthy. However, he then went and blew it all when he was 22 by taking as his third wife Myra Gale Brown... his thirteen-year-old cousin once-removed. The scandal resulted in tour cancellations and his being blacklisted by most radio stations.

Lewis remained in the wilderness for many years but made something of a comeback with the release of his album *Live at the Star Club, Hamburg*, described by one critic as "Extraordinary — the purest, hardest rock & roll ever committed to record".

The rest of Lewis' life has been as wild as his piano-playing. Two of his wives died in accidents as did two of his sons; he accidentally shot his bass-player in the chest with a Magnum; and in 1976 he was arrested in Graceland after ramming the gates of Elvis' mansion, leaping from his car with a gun and telling a startled guard that he was "there to shoot Elvis".

Always one to make statement, he also set fire to his piano at the end of one set in protest at being billed below Chuck Berry.

Incidentally, Jerry Lee was another who dedicated his music to the Dark Side:

"IT'S STRANGE, THE SAME MUSIC THAT THEY KICKED ME OUT OF SCHOOL FOR IS THE SAME KIND OF MUSIC THEY PLAY IN THEIR CHURCHES TODAY. THE DIFFERENCE IS, I KNOW I AM PLAYING FOR THE DEVIL AND THEY DON'T."

Ted Nugent, Nikki Sixx and Tommy Lee

You know straight away that any story involving these three characters cannot be good. You are correct. Hold onto your lunch readers, it's going to get ugly.

Ted's Story ....

For those of you not familiar with Ted Nugent, he made his musical mark as a hard rock musician in the '70s and early '80s. Since then his musical career has gone down faster than George Michael in a public toilet (I know, George Michael overkill, I'll rein it in...), while his crazed right-wing rhetoric has reached stratospheric proportions. A self-avowed patriot of the Good ol' US of A and major supporter of all Republican causes, Nugent evidently didn't feel the need to actually go and fight for his country himself. In a 1976 interview with *High Times* magazine, he confessed that he had gone to extreme measures to avoid the draft to Vietnam. For a month before his medical he stopped brushing his teeth, brushing his hair or bathing. Concerned that a little general filth might not do the trick, he decided to take it up a notch or two. In the week before the interview he decided to cut out the middleman and used his pants as a toilet. That's right — brave patriot Ted Nugent actually peed and crapped his pants to avoid the draft. The plan worked:

"... in the mail I got this big juicy 4-F. They'd call dead people before they'd call me... I just wasn't into it. I was too busy doin' my own thing."

Things such as writing a best-selling song called *Cat Scratch Fever*. Now I wonder where the inspiration for that particular song came from?

A variation on this theme concerns Nikki Sixx and Tommy Lee of Motley Crue and... The Spaghetti Incident

For some undisclosed reason (probably to avoid a war somewhere), Nikki Sixx and Tommy Lee decided to have a competition to see who could go the longest without any form of bathing and still get groupies to sleep with them. For most people this would be seriously gross and irresponsible but in their case they were on tour and performing every night... on stage and off it. Talk about blood, sweat and tears... yes, those groupies must have seen it all!

After two months (you read correctly my friend... two long months) Nikki Sixx finally admitted defeat when a young and obviously enthusiastic fan dived down to inspect his lower microphone and promptly vomited all over his tackle. Evidently she had enjoyed a pre-concert dining experience at a local Italian joint and thereafter it became known among polite society as... **The Spaghetti Incident!**

Bebe Buell ....

Bad behaviour is by no means limited to the boys. Bebe Buell is a singer, model and the November 1974 Playboy Playmate of the month. The Cameron Crowe film *Almost Famous* is reportedly based on the lives of Bebe Buell and Pennie Trumbull, two of history's greatest groupies. Bebe had relationships with Iggy Pop, Todd Rundgren, Jimmy Page, David Bowie, Elvis Costello and Rod Stewart. It is also well known that she is the mother of actress Liv Tyler, the father being Aerosmith front man and *American Idol* mouthpiece, Steve Tyler. Bebe clearly had a thing for Men With Mouths, since she dated both Jagger and Tyler. The notoriously possessive Jagger was even heard to complain once, " Why do you want the fake Mick when you've got the real one?"

Bebe published an extremely revealing and best-selling autobiography *Rebel Heart: An American Rock and Roll Journey*, in which she claimed, **"I WAS NEVER ON A QUEST FOR SEX ITSELF. IN FACT, TO ME, IT'S THE HARDEST PART OF A RELATIONSHIP. I WAS ALWAYS ON A QUEST FOR ROCK 'N' ROLL."**

Of course you were Bebe... and where better to start looking than inside Mick Jagger's pants?

Ozzy Osbourne ··························

It's easy to laugh at Ozzy Osbourne as he stumbles and swears his way through MTV's most popular show ever — *The Osbournes.* But Ozzy is a man with some serious personal demons… maybe literally.

In 2002, he was given his own star on the Hollywood Walk of Fame. Marilyn Manson introduced Ozzy with the words,

> **"THIS STAR RIGHT HERE PROVES THAT IT'S QUITE OBVIOUS THAT OZZY HAS MANAGED TO SUCCEED WHILE REMAINING INSANE AND STRANGELY HAPPY, DESPITE HIS VARIOUS CRIMES AGAINST GOD AND NATURE."**

In fact, during the time that *The Osbournes* became a household hit, Ozzy and his dysfunctional family were feted by many of the great and the good, including President Bush in the White House, who declared "The thing about Ozzy is, he's made a lot of big hit recordings — *Party With the Animals*, *Sabbath Bloody Sabbath*, *Facing Hell*, *Black Skies* and *Bloodbath in Paradise*… Ozzy, Mom loves your stuff." Even Dan Quayle described *The Osbournes* as representing "good entertainment" and "good family values". Which episodes was he watching?

Can this be the same Ozzy Osbourne that has incurred the wrath of Church and animal rights groups all around the world for his various outrageous acts?

The song *Black Sabbath*, in which Ozzy sings of a smiling Satan appearing as a black shape with eyes of fire, was taken from an actual, demonic visitation of Sabbath bassist Geezer Butler.

"Having borrowed a 16th century tome of black magic from [Ozzy] Osbourne one afternoon, Butler awoke that night to find a black shape staring balefully at him from the foot of his bed. After a few frightening moments, the figure slowly vanished into thin air... I told Ozzy about it. It stuck in his mind, and when we started playing 'Black Sabbath', he just came out with those lyrics... It had to come out, and it eventually did in that song — and then there was only one possible name for the band, really!'"

In 1978, due to his heavy drug and alcohol addiction, Ozzy Osbourne was fired as the lead singer of Black Sabbath. He was saved from oblivion by his wife Sharon who took over his career and relaunched him onto a grateful world. In case anyone doubted it, he told *Hit Parader* magazine in 1981: "... let everybody know that I'm just as evil and just as crazy as ever."

To prove his point he pulled a number of bizarre onstage stunts. During one concert, a devoted fan hurled a bat onto the stage: "I thought it was a toy. It must have been stunned by the lights because it looked dead when I picked it up. I put it in my mouth as a joke. Its wings started flapping and I ripped it out of my mouth but its head came off!" Unfortunately for Ozzy, the bat had the last laugh as he needed two weeks of intensely painful rabies jabs to guard against... (OK, but would anyone really have noticed if Ozzy Osbourne had contracted rabies?)

As Sharon was resurrecting Ozzy's career, she set up a meeting between Ozzy and CBS Records executives. To start the meeting, Sharon planned for Ozzy to release three white doves as a peace offering. Ozzy released two of the doves then seemed to decide the gesture was all a bit too sentimental and nauseating and so he bit the head off the third.

> "THEN I WENT CHOMP, SPIT. THE DOVE'S HEAD LANDED ON THE PR CHICK'S LAP IN A SPLATTER OF BLOOD. TO BE HONEST WITH YOU, I WAS SO PISSED, IT JUST TASTED OF COINTREAU. WELL, COINTREAU AND FEATHERS... AND A BIT OF BEAK."

In 1982 while in San Antonio, Texas, Sharon found him in their room in a horrible state. Deciding that he was in no fit state to go anywhere, she hid his clothes to prevent him from leaving the hotel. Not to be outdone, Ozzy slipped on his wife's evening dress and high heels, hobbled over the road and was arrested when he was found peeing against a memorial to the heroes of the Alamo. He was forbidden to perform in San Antonio for the next ten years.

That was also the year that the romantic Ozzy proposed to Sharon: "Shortly after Randy died (an accident in which members of his band and entourage died when the plane they were in crashed into the tour bus) I asked Sharon to marry me. She said yes. So I put a ring on her finger, and we set a date. Then the booze wore off and I changed my mind. It went on like that for months. We had more engagements than most people have wedding guests. I proposed to her 17 times in the end."

Most people would settle down into some form of midlife, marital bliss. Not Ozzy. Rolling Stone magazine describes some of Ozzy's wildest acts: **"… HE HAS SHOT UP A HENHOUSE FULL OF CHICKENS AND KILLED A WHOLE GANG OF CATS AND SNORTED A LINE OF ANTS LIKE THEY WERE A LINE OF COCAINE AND BITTEN THE HEAD OFF A BAT, AND CATAPULTED MEAT (STOMACH AND INTESTINES, MOSTLY) INTO HIS AUDIENCE."**

All true! During Ozzy's *Diary of a Madman* concerts, Ozzy would toss raw cow livers and pig intestines into the audience. In fact it was in his contract with the tour promoter that he must provide at least 25 pounds of raw cow livers and pig intestines for his "raw meat" baptism.

Ozzy on his version of *Cats*, the musical: "I was taking drugs so much I was a wreck. The final straw came when I shot all our cats. We had about 17, and I went crazy and shot them all. My wife found me under the piano in a white suit, a shotgun in one hand and a knife in the other."

"I really wish I knew why I've done some of the things I've done over the years. Sometimes I think that I'm possessed by some outside spirit. A few years ago, I was convinced of that — I thought I truly was possessed by the devil. I remember sitting through *The Exorcist* a dozen times, saying to myself, 'Yeah, I can relate to that'."

Ozzy has made no secret of the fact that has been obsessed with violence and killing for most of his life: "I'm one of these guys, I wake up in the morning and got a fuckin' problem: I'm looking for something to kill or blow up or some fuckin' thing..."

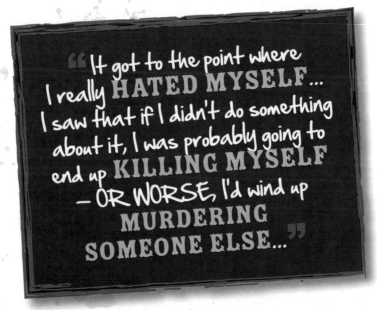

"It got to the point where I really HATED MYSELF... I saw that if I didn't do something about it, I was probably going to end up KILLING MYSELF — OR WORSE, I'd wind up MURDERING SOMEONE ELSE..."

In fact, Ozzy's predictions almost came true on 2 September, 1989 when Ozzy did indeed try to murder his wife. Sharon described the moment to Barbara Walters on *20/20* in 2002: "I was downstairs reading. He came down with just his underpants on. And he's like, 'We've come to a decision.' And I'm like, 'We've?' And he said, 'You have to die'. And then he just dived on me and got me down on the floor and was just strangling me. But he was gone. There was blinkers on his eyes. He had gone. It wasn't Ozzy."

Ozzy was arrested for attempted murder. "The worst thing I did was trying to kill Sharon. I got busted for strangling her and when I woke up in prison I didn't have a clue why I was there. When the policeman read me the charge, I freaked out." According to the police report, Ozzy's first words on waking up in the cell were "But I was in a Chinese restaurant five minutes ago!"

After recovering from the shock Sharon decided to drop all charges, made him go to rehab and has stayed happily married to him ever since. Sure brings a tear to the eye...

Snoop Dogg ....

I know what you're thinking — surely not Snoop Dogg, laidback silvery-tongued rapper, model father and star of *Snoop Dogg's Father Hood*? Yes folks I am indeed talking about Calvin Broadus — former porn-star (*Snoop Dogg's Doggystyle* and *Girls Gone Wild Doggy Style*), acquitted murderer, acclaimed actor and best-selling rapper. While the Ozbourne's TV show was a never-ending stream of arguments and swearing, Mr Dogg has a much more laidback approach. Surely this has nothing to do with his enormous consumption of weed (named Stoner of the Year 2002 by *High Times* magazine). You have to admire a man who comes up with episode headlines such as *Snoop It Like Beckham*; *The Doggs and the Bees*; and *The Dogg Whisperer*. However, the Dogg's life has not always been one of such domestic bliss.

Snoop grew up in a tough part of Long Beach, California. As a teenager he joined the notorious Rollin' 20 Crips gang and was constantly in trouble with the police. In a *Playboy* interview in 1995, he said:

"I don't know anybody who joined a gang for protection. That shit doesn't happen in my hood. You join it because you need love and family support. You need a motherfucker who can identify with what you're going through."

Snoop was a key figure in the development of '90s Gangsta Rap with his album *Doggy Style*. Rappers usually rap about love, sex, violence, socio-political issues, crime, race and street life. The problem was that the street life started to encroach a little too closely on the music itself. In the mid-1990s, a rivalry between the East Coast and West Coast rappers in the US broke out into a full-on battle. The focal points of the feud were West Coast-based rapper **2Pac** (and his label Death Row Records) and East Coast-based rapper **The Notorious B.I.G.** (and his label Bad Boy Records), both of whom were murdered. Other rappers who took the whole street thing a bit too far included **Slick Rick Walters** who attempted to murder of his cousin; Dasean Cooper, also known as **J-Dee** of Da Lench Mob, serving 29 years to life for the murder of his girlfriend's male roommate; and **Flavor Flav** of Public Enemy who served three months in jail for firing a gun at a neighbour.

Snoop started life as a hoodlum in the ghettos of Long Beach and was no stranger to drugs and the law. One interesting snippet is that Snoop went to the same high school as Cameron Diaz. Not only that, the doe-eyed beauty is convinced she remembers buying weed from him. "We went to high school together, he was a year older than me... He was very tall and skinny and wore lots of ponytails in his hair and I'm pretty sure I got weed from him."

After graduating from high school, his life selling cocaine on the streets came to a halt when he was arrested for possession.

"IN JAIL, YOU'RE EITHER GONNA BE THE TOUGHEST MOTHERFUCKER, OR YOU GONNA BE THE SOFTEST MOTHERFUCKER, OR YOU GOTTA FIND SOME OTHER SHIT TO BE."

He was sentenced to three years in prison and upon his release, tried to avoid trouble by concentrating on his music. "As a black man, you definitely have to be cocky, but not conceited. You got to have that kind of swagger, 'cause there's so much against you, and there's so many people that's just as good as you, if not better than you. You gotta push a little harder to make yourself shine."

Snoop has an interesting place in the pantheon of wild musicians. Most of his predecessors started off with fairly dull, middle-class lives and proceeded to lose the plot as they became wealthier and more famous. Snoop started life wild and used music as a way of saving himself from the gangs and violence of Los Angeles. He hasn't exactly conformed entirely, but he has become a father figure to many gang members in the States.

"It's just a matter of communication. An argument or dispute is a conversation away from peace. It's just a matter of who is going to be man enough to say 'I was wrong' or 'I'm willing to hear what you're saying' instead of jumping to conclusions and wanting to fight and hurt somebody. That's not the mentality that I push and promote. That's why I'm so successful because peace is my main thing, it's not about money. It's about making sure everybody is having a good time and loving and living and enjoying life."

Keith Moon ·

If Keith Richards is the final word in excessive behavior among the living, the honour among the fallen must go to Keith Moon, a man so mad his nickname was "**The Loon**". An early school report described him as "Retarded artistically, idiotic in other respects". Clearly the man who wrote his report card never saw the man in action. Keith playing the drums was like nothing before or since. The only other drummer to come close to his playing style was **Animal**, the crazed drummer in the Muppet Show's band Dr Teeth and the Electric Mayhem. Hidden behind one of rock 'n' roll's largest drum kits, Keith wouldn't so much play the drums as attack them. With a line-up of front men that included Roger Daltrey, Pete Townshend and John Entwistle, it would have been easy for a drummer with *The Who* to disappear into the background. Instead, he almost became a show within the show.

The Who were always one of the '60s class acts with an extraordinarily talented line-up. At one of their concerts they had problems throughout the night with feedback from one of the speakers. Towards the end of the show, Pete Townshend attacked the problematic amp in sheer frustration. Never one to miss an opportunity, the Loon took this as his cue to smash up his entire drum kit. And so it became The Who's prerogative to smash up their instruments at the end

> **Keith Moon, God rest his soul, once drove his car through the glass doors of a hotel, driving all the way up to the reception desk, got out and asked for the key to his room.**
>
> — Pete Townshend, The Who, 2005

of their concerts. For most people this would be enough: "Wow — look how wild we are, we've smashed up our instruments." But for The Loon, enough was never enough.

When the band appeared on an American TV show called *The Smothers Brothers Comedy Hour* (don't ask me — I have no idea why a band as cool as The Who would appear on such a show), the Loon decided to spice up the final melee by putting explosives inside the drums. Unfortunately for everyone else in the room, The Loon had no idea how much explosives to use. Being incapable of erring on the side of caution, he erred instead on the side of excess. The final explosion was so powerful that the Loon ended up on his back with pieces of shrapnel from his cymbals embedded in his body; Pete Townshend was blown off the stage, his hair on fire and with permanent damage to his hearing; while offstage guest star Bette Davis was said to have fainted and been treated for shock.

But it wasn't just The Loon's onstage antics that made him so memorable. His entire life was like one continuous stage performance. Despite coming from a fairly working class background in London, he decided to adopt a ludicrous crusty English accent and would say things like "It must be time for drinky-poos." Sadly for the Loon, it always seemed to be time for either drinky-poos or druggy-poos and its effects started to show. His consumption was easily on a par with Mr Richards but he didn't handle it quite as well as Keef. He started to get paunchy and his behavior became more and more erratic.

He loved dressing up in fancy-dress and would regularly be found hanging out with friends dressed as the Pope. Not everyone found his behavior entertaining. The Loon's neighbor in Malibu was the King of Cool, *Steve McQueen*. After McQueen had reported The Loon to the police a few times for disruptive behaviour and built a high wall between the properties, Keith decided to take his revenge.

He took a cue from McQueen's classic film *The Great Escape* and built a large ramp up the side of the wall with the intent of leaping over the wall to surprise his neighbour. Before he could make the leap however, The Loon decided on a better way to extract his revenge. He dressed up as Hitler, knocked on McQueen's door and when McQueen opened it he got down on all fours and bit McQueen's dog.

By 1978 the Loon's behaviour and drumming had become so erratic that The Who were looking to replace him. However, in the early hours of 6 September The Loon and his partner returned from a Paul McCartney party and watched a video of Vincent Price's *The Abominable Dr Phibes*, took some sleeping pills and relaxants and went to bed. A few hours later, he woke up and prepared a breakfast of steak and champagne. Obviously deciding he needed something to help him sleep some more, he took another handful of relaxants and went to bed, never to rise again.

So there you have it, folks. Depending on which way you look at it, music can either be the catalyst for a life of excess and debauchery, a ticket to an early curtain call, a road to salvation or a passage to a large dry-cleaning bill. Keith is probably one of the few that has run through all these rites of passage (with the exception of death, which he somehow manages to keep at arm's length) and come out the other side in relatively good shape. As philosophical as ever, Keith should have the final word:

"THERE IS SOMETHING INSIDE ME THAT JUST WANTS TO EXCITE THAT THING IN OTHER PEOPLE, BECAUSE I KNOW IT'S THERE IN EVERYBODY.

There's a demon in me, and there's a demon in everybody else. I get a uniquely ridiculous response — the skulls flow in by the truckload, sent by well-wishers. People love that image. They imagined me, they made me, the folks out there created this folk hero. Bless their hearts. And I'll do the best I can to fulfill their needs. They're wishing me to do things that they can't. They've got to do this job, they've got this life, they're an insurance salesman... but at the same time, inside of them is a raging Keith Richards. When you talk of a folk hero, they've written the script for you and you better fulfill it. And I did my best. It's no exaggeration that I was basically living like an outlaw. And I got into it! I knew that I was on everybody's list. All I had to do was recant and I'd be all right. But that was something I just couldn't do."

HOW TO BE WILD

Clearly a family history of mental instability would help. Philip Larkin's poem *They Fuck You Up Your Mom & Dad* could be a homily for all budding rock stars. Of course you would have to throw in the insidious influence of alcohol, drugs, too many late nights, hanging out late with the wrong kind of groupie... all the things that make up a psychiatrist's wet-dream. When it comes to bad influences, musicians just can't get enough of them. Bad is the new good.

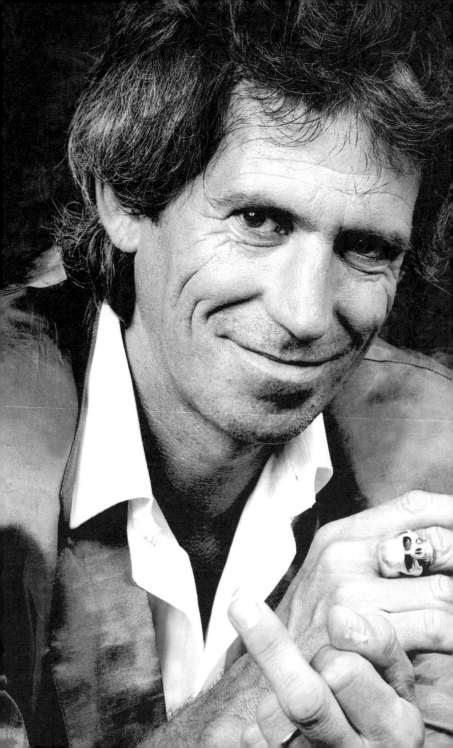

In 1981, Keith told *New York Times* music critic Robert Palmer: "I've been to hear Jerry Lee Lewis and Fats Domino recently and they're playing as great as ever. I intend to be like them. I'll be out there playing if they have to wheel me out in a wheelchair."

Keith isn't quite at that stage yet (although he has been in the past), but the years are starting to take their toll almost as much as his excessive lifestyle. He may look like something scary from the Halloween box, but his talent remains undimmed.

Keith: "As you go down the pike you realise that in musical terms and as far as musicians and music goes, there's a weird community. You realise that at the end of the day, a musician's gravestone, the best thing it can read is that 'Hey, he passed it on'. And you know, when other guys younger than me come up to me, you realise that you're just a part of a long process of troubadours and minstrels and balladeers and storytellers and it goes back forever. In a way, you get the strange feeling that you're part of this weird fraternity... you get this wonderful feeling of continuity, going all the way back through the mists of time. And you're just one of those guys that told a story and kept them happy and sang a song and they took care of you too, for the pleasure of business."

The Rolling Stones were once seen as the complete anti-establishment band. But time has mellowed them and they are now recognised as being something intrinsically British, almost an institution in themselves. This was confirmed in 2003 when Mick Jagger was knighted for Services to Music. Charlie Watts was quoted in *According to the Rolling*

Stones as saying, "Anybody else would be lynched: 18 wives and 20 children and he's knighted, fantastic!"

However, the honour didn't sit well with all members of the band. Keith was horrified that Mick decided to accept the "fucking paltry honour" and said that he did not want to take the stage with someone wearing a "coronet and sporting the old ermine. It's not what the Stones is about, is it?".

Mick's response was typical of the thick-lipped one:

"I THINK HE WOULD PROBABLY LIKE TO GET THE SAME HONOUR HIMSELF. IT'S LIKE BEING GIVEN AN ICE CREAM — ONE GETS ONE AND THEY ALL WANT ONE. IT'S NOTHING NEW. KEITH LIKES TO MAKE A FUSS."

However, Keith also has his iconoclastic moments. In 2008 he starred in Louis Vuitton's classic advertising campaign, photographed by the equally iconoclastic Annie Liebovitz. Said Antoine Arnault of Louis Vuitton: "Keith Richards needs absolutely no introduction. He is a global icon, an inspiration to millions, and we are honoured that — after Mikhail Gorbachev, Katherine Deneuve, Steffi Graff and Andre Agassi — he has agreed to represent Louis Vuitton. This is the first time ever that Keith Richards has participated in an advertising campaign of any sort, and it is hard to imagine a more compelling embodiment of a personal, emotional journey."

"Life sucks, but in a beautiful kind of way."
— Axl Rose of Guns`n` Roses,1998

It is true that Keith has been on one hell of a journey. One that few others would be as well equipped to survive. He is the Ernest Shackleton of Rock 'n' Roll — going where others fear to tread, or maybe more of a James T. Kirk going "Where No Man Has Gone Before" while being simultaneously lost in space.

Each time you wonder what else he could possibly do with his life, he surprises you with another cameo appearance. Quite literally, as it turned out in the 2007 film *Pirates of the Caribbean: At World's End.* Johnny Depp had let slip that he had based the performance of his character, Jack Sparrow, on Keith Richards. So when the time came to appoint someone to play his father in the film, who could be better suited for the part?

"I thought of Keith because I was trying to figure out what pirates might have been like, their lifestyle back in the eighteenth century, and I thought, oh man, they were the rock 'n' roll stars of the era. On the road to some degree, freedom, adventure, women, outlaw behavior, all of that stuff. And you see the greatest rock 'n' roll star of all time, there are so many options, but to me it's Keith Richards hands down..."

"... Part of it was that Keith was the sage, the wise, unbelievably smart guy. It's kind of like Hunter Thompson, who is a brilliant writer and a great man, I've seen it happen where people, because they look at Hunter and they think he's out of it, so they just assume that he's just burnt and he's not lucid, and they've been kind of disrespectful in a very roundabout way, and Hunter being incredibly smart, he'll pin-point, and I've see him just level them verbally, just decimate them, and I think Keith is similar. Yeah, people just assume Keith Richards — oh yeah, the junkie years in the '70s, and he's out of it and all the stuff, but no, no, no, he's one of the most well read, brilliant people I've ever come into contact with. He knows everything about everything — a history buff, history to the letter. It wasn't an imitation of Keith or anything like that. It was just like a salute to him, and beyond the fact that I think that he's the greatest rock 'n' roll star of all times, I also think that he's an incredibly interesting man beyond the rock and roll, beyond the Stones. He's unbelievably wise. He's really a wise man, a sage, a Buddha or something..."

When the coolest man in Hollywood refers to you as "a sage, a Buddha", you know that you must have done something right with your life. So Keith, the man who scared the crap out of western society for a decade, who wasn't expected to live beyond the '70s, who has never undergone a Madonna makeover, has become the King of the Wild Things as well as the King of Cool. The man is timeless, as are the Rolling Stones.

As Keith himself put it: **"YOU'VE GOT THE SUN, YOU'VE GOT THE MOON, AND YOU'VE GOT THE ROLLING STONES."**

THE ROLLING STONES DISCOGRAPHY

Rarities 1971–2003 (2005)

A Bigger Bang (2005)

Singles 1968–1971 (2005)

Live Licks (UK version) (2004)

Live Licks (US Version) (2004)

Jump Back: The Best of The Rolling Stones (2004)

Singles 1965–1967 (2004)

Singles 1963–1965 (2004)

Sympathy For The Devil – Remix (2003)

Forty Licks (2002)

Flashpoint (2000)

No Security (1998)

Bridges To Babylon (1997)

Rock & Roll Circus (1996)

Stripped (1995)

Rolling Stones Rock And Roll Circus (1995)

Voodoo Lounge (1994)

Who Are The Stones? (1993)

Flashpoint + Collectibles (1991)

Singles Collection: The London Years (1989)

Steel Wheels (1989)

Singles Collection... (1989)

Dirty Work (1986)

Rewind (1971–1984) (1984)

Undercover (1983)

Still Life (1982)

Tattoo You (1981)

Sucking In The Seventies (1981)

Emotional Rescue (1980)

Some Girls (1978)

Love You Live (1977)

Black And Blue (1976)

Made In The Shade (1975)

Metamorphosis (1975)

It's Only Rock & Roll (1974)

Goats Head Soup (1973)

More Hot Rocks (Big Hits & Fazed Cookies) (1972)

Exile On Main St. (1972)

Exile On Main Street (1994) (1972)

Sticky Fingers (1971)

Hot Rocks 1964-1971 (1971)

Sticky Fingers (1994) (1971)

Get Yer Ya-Ya's Out! (1970)

Let It Bleed (1969)

Through The Past Darkly (Big Hits Vol. 2) (1969)

Through The Past... (1969)

Beggars Banquet (1968)

Their Satanic Majesties Request (1967)

Flowers (1967)

Between The Buttons (1967)

Big Hits (High Tide And Green Grass) (1966)

Aftermath (1966)

Got LIVE If You Want It! (1966)

Out Of Our Heads (1965)

The Rolling Stones, Now! (1965)

December's Children (And Everybody's) (1965)

England's Newest Hit Makers (1964)

The Rolling Stones (1964)

12 x 5 (1964)

ABOUT THE AUTHOR

Jack Wilson was born in England but in his early twenties set off around the world looking for romance, adventure and decent food. After travelling through Europe, South America and the US he ended up in Asia where he lives today. With his dashing good looks and easy charm he is often mistaken for George Clooney's smarter, wittier, more sophisticated and better-endowed younger brother.

Jack is a child of the '80s punk era and a keen drummer. Many have questioned his ability to hold a beat but Jack prefers to think that he thrashes out rhythms that other drummers are simply unable to find.

A writer and publisher by profession, Jack can be reached for sage advice, words of wisdom, a decent malt whisky and a Cuban cigar at 3fingersof jack@gmail.com.

SOURCES

Chris Campion, *The Observer*, 20 February 2005

Dave Hunt, *America: The Sorcerers New Apprentice*,
    Eugene, OR: Harvest House, 1988

Robert Greenfield, *Exile on Main St.: A Season in Hell with the
    Rolling Stones*, Cambridge, MA: Da Capo Press, 2006

Stephen Davis, *Hammer of the Gods: The Led Zeppelin Saga*,
    New York: Berkley Boulevard Books, 1995

The Rolling Stones, *According to the Rolling Stones*,
    San Francisco, CA: Chronicle Books

Victor Bockris, *Keith Richards: The Biography*,
    Cambridge, MA: Da Capo Press, 2003

www.accessmylibrary.com/article-1G1-165363972/
    virtuosity-violin-devil-really.html

www.bluntreview.com/reviews/depp.htm

www.classicbands.com/
    AndrewLoogOldhamInterview.html

www.dovesong.com/Positive_music/
    plant_experiments.ssp

www.homepages.spa.umn.edu/
    ~duvernoi/satan.htm